We Win!

We Win!

Literal Commentary and Study Guide
on the
Book of Revelation

Reverend Barry F. Brinson

WESTBOW
PRESS®
A DIVISION OF THOMAS NELSON
& ZONDERVAN

WestBow Press books may be ordered through booksellers or by contacting:

WestBow Press
A Division of Thomas Nelson & Zondervan
1663 Liberty Drive
Bloomington, IN 47403
www.westbowpress.com
1 (866) 928-1240

Because of the dynamic nature of the Internet, any web addresses or links contained in this book may have changed since publication and may no longer be valid. The views expressed in this work are solely those of the author and do not necessarily reflect the views of the publisher, and the publisher hereby disclaims any responsibility for them.

"Scripture taken from the NEW AMERICAN STANDARD BIBLE®,
© Copyright 1960, 1962, 1963, 1968, 1971, 1972, 1973,
1975, 1977, 1995 by The Lockman Foundation
Used by permission" (www.Lockman.org)

Any people depicted in stock imagery provided by Thinkstock are models, and such images are being used for illustrative purposes only. Certain stock imagery © Thinkstock.

ISBN: 978-1-5127-3058-6 (sc)
ISBN: 978-1-5127-3060-9 (hc)
ISBN: 978-1-5127-3059-3 (e)

Print information available on the last page.

WestBow Press rev. date: 03/03/2016

CONTENTS

PREFACE

We Win is a down to earth commentary on the book of Revelation. God's Word is revealed using a common sense literal interpretation. God's Word is holy, inspired, infallible, and inerrant. Therefore, God's Word can be expected to be true all of the time. John writes in the book of Revelation, "I testify to everyone who hears the Words of the prophecy of this book: if anyone adds to them, God will add to him the plagues which are written in this book; and if anyone takes away from the words of the book of this prophecy, God will take away his part from the tree of life and from the holy city, which are written in this book." (Rev. 22:18-19)

The book of Revelation is not intended to be embellished with abstract ideas or notions. It is to be understood. "The Revelation of Jesus, which God gave Him to show to His bondservants, the things which must soon take place." (Revelation 1:1) God desires that His Word concerning the end times will be understood. There is no special code needed, there is no hidden meaning, and it is not intended just for those of high intellect. Because there are no special codes and there is no hidden meaning, "We Win!" takes the book of Revelation to mean just what it says. The interpretation is literal and the language is easy to understand. This book is for everyone who wants to know what God's plan for the future is and how that plan will be executed. Hear and understand how God plans to bring an end to this world of sin and evil and how He will recreate a New Heaven and New Earth where righteousness dwells. In the end, "We Win!"

PROLOGUE

I am writing this book because the book of Revelation is meant to be understood. Revelation is God's plan for the future and God desires for us to know what the future will be. Revelation is not some cryptic message that requires decoding or deciphering in order to get to the truth. It says exactly what it means. When we approach Revelation with the idea that it must be deciphered or decoded the message takes on a variety of meanings depending on the method used for decoding. Many people have taken this approach today leaving us with so many different interpretations that people can decide for themselves what they want Revelation to say and can find someone somewhere who says what they want to hear. The problem is that once we decide that God's Word is not to be taken literally we can impose upon it anything we want. This is not true of just the book of Revelation but it is true with all Scripture. Many theologians deny and distort Scripture. From the very beginning, in Genesis, they deny the six day creation. These same people will deny that Job was a real person, claim that a worldwide flood was impossible, show how the parting of the Red Sea was a simple natural occurrence, they deny the virgin birth of Jesus, and mock His resurrection. In fact, these same people spin a yarn so far out of sync with God's Word that it is almost believable.

In the following pages I will attempt to put no restrictions on God or on what He can and cannot do. I will attempt to bring a literal interpretation to the book of Revelation and show that God has not hidden His truth from us but desires that we all come to understand His plan for His people.

I hope you find comfort in God's plan for your future. If not, then perhaps you need to consider your personal relationship to God. God's plan is to destroy all evil and establish a place for His people where they can live in peace and comfort, void of all evil and hatred and disappointments. The old order of things will have passed away and there will be no more death or mourning or crying or pain. God's future plan for His people is a New Heaven and New Earth where God will dwell with His people. He will wipe away every tear from their eyes. God's new creation will be one of love, joy, peace, and happiness.

"The Spirit of the bride says, 'Come!' And let him who hears say, 'Come!' Whoever is thirsty, let him come; and whoever wishes, let him take the free gift of the water of life without cost." (Rev. 22:17)

Introduction

The book of Revelation is the culmination of God's creation. The Bible begins with the creation of the present earth and everything in it. All things were created perfect. Adam and Eve walked with God and God provided for their every need. They were at peace with all creation. There were no weeds to destroy the garden. They walked side by side with the "wild" animals without fear. There were no storms, earthquakes, tornados or hurricanes. There was nothing in God's creation to bring sadness, death, crying or pain. And "then by the sin of one man sin entered the world and death through sin and death spread to all men because all sinned." (Rom. 13:12) God created the earth and everything in it perfect and holy. Then, after only one thousand years the world becomes so corrupt that no righteous person could be found. God decides to destroy all He has created. "But Noah found favor in the sight of the Lord." (Gen. 6:8). God chooses Noah and his family to save out of the initial purging of the earth by the flood. After another thousand years all the people turned to idol worship. So God chooses Abram to be His. "No longer shall your name be called Abram, but your name shall be Abraham; for I have made you a father of a multitude of nations." (Gen. 17:5) After another thousand years the people were not satisfied being ruled by God. They wanted a king. So God chose David to be a king over them. And then, after another thousand years, God sends His Son to earth to redeem His people from the bonds of Satan.

God, in one final act, accomplished what no one was able to do. He sent His son, Jesus, to live a perfect life, without sin. Even though Jesus had no fault in Him, He was condemned to die. Jesus, because of His perfect life, earned the right to die for all. Jesus brought salvation to people of every tribe, nation, people, and tongue through His death and resurrection. The penalty of sin is death. The penalty must be paid. Jesus' death on the cross paid the penalty for all. Any and all who accept Christ as their Lord and Savior are redeemed through His blood.

God's plan for the future unfolds before our very eyes as we read through the Bible. Scripture focuses on the gathering of God's people together in order that they may inhabit the New Earth which is yet to be created. God is perfect and holy and therefore He will not let anyone or anything come into His presence that is not perfect and holy. God will dwell with His people on the New Earth, therefore the New Earth and its inhabitants must be void of all sin and evil.

God is the same today, yesterday and tomorrow. His plan for the future has not changed. Salvation has never been by being a descendent of Noah, or being a child of Abraham, or being a citizen of the kingdom of David but it is through the grace and mercy of God who gathers together for Himself a people to be His children. And these people, people of every tribe and nation and people and tongue, whom God chooses, will be the residents in the final kingdom of God.

All the earth must be purged of evil and sin in order for God to accomplish His purpose. The book of Revelation is about God's final call to redemption, His judgment of those who refuse to repent, the total annihilation of everything and everyone who is wicked and evil, and the establishment of a New Heaven and a New Earth devoid of all evil and sin.

The book of Revelation refers to two classes of people, there are believers, those who dwell in heaven and there are unbelievers, those who dwell on earth. The believers are those who have accepted Christ as their Lord and Savior. Some have already died and their souls are in heaven with Jesus. Some will die a natural death or will be martyred because of their testimony. And some will live to be caught up in the cloud when Jesus returns. The unbelievers are those who put their faith and trust in worldly things. Some have already died and their souls are in Hades waiting the resurrection of judgment. Some will die before the tribulation begins and they too will lie in wait of judgment. And some will be destroyed in the tribulation and the wrath of God when He brings His final judgment on the whole earth.

The book of Revelation is "Good News" for the believers who dwell in the heavenly realm but not so good for those who "dwell on earth." I hope that as you read this you are among the believers and find comfort knowing that at last God's purpose will be accomplished and we will live in a perfect world void of all evil and sin and there will be no more crying or death or pain. The first things will have passed away. We will have won the victory and will stand in the very presence of the living God. He will be our God and we will be His people forever and ever.

Overview

The book of Revelation is the climax to the Bible. Everything in the Bible points to the final destruction of all evil and the establishment of God's new kingdom. Like a good mystery novel the story is not complete until the last chapter when the victims have been avenged and the culprit is brought to justice. Revelation is the final "chapter" of the Bible. Everyone has been attacked and abused by Satan since the very beginning of time. The book of Revelation brings the story to a close. Finally, after thousands of years, Satan and his followers are brought to justice and thrown into the lake of fire. Satan's victims, who have remained faithful to God, are rewarded. They are given white robes and golden crowns and provided a new place to live where righteousness reigns. God provides them with everything they need and want. There is peace on earth and good will towards all men.

The Bible can only be truly and completely understood in light of the book of Revelation. The book of Revelation can only be truly and completely understood in light of the entire Bible. It is when we understand the theme of the Bible that Revelation makes sense. And it is when we understand the outcome of God's work in Revelation that we are able to grasp the importance of the things that lead up to the Revelation. Therefore, in preparation of our study of Revelation we will begin with an overview of Scripture exploring the theme of the Bible. This will be followed by an overview of the book of Revelation.

OVERVIEW OF SCRIPTURE

What is the Bible? The Bible is God's Word. It is holy, inspired, infallible, and inerrant. That is, it is set aside for God's purpose. The Bible is not a common book for a common purpose. The Bible is holy. The Bible is God's voice to us. God speaks as we read and study the Bible. The Bible is recorded by man through the power and inspiration of the Holy Spirit. "All Scripture is inspired by God and profitable for teaching, for reproof, for correction, for training in righteousness so that the man of God may be adequate, equipped for every good work." (2 Tim. 3:16). In the original Greek the Word "inspired" is actually "God breathed." All Scripture is God breathed, out of the very mouth of God. God's Word is true and cannot be proven false. God's Word is infallible. All of the information in the Bible is true, from the six day creation, to the world wide flood, to the parting of the Red Sea, to the virgin birth of Jesus, to the resurrection of Jesus, to the final destruction of this earth and recreation of the New Heavens and New Earth. The Bible speaks the truth from start to finish. There are no errors in the Bible. The Bible is inerrant. That is, in the original text the Bible has no errors. Any inconsistencies or errors found in the Bible have been introduced by man through the various translations. The further we get away from the original text the more errors we will have. Therefore, for serious study, we should use a translation that is word-for-word and based on the oldest manuscripts available. These word-for-word translations are sometimes harder to read and understand than thought-for-thought translations or paraphrased Bibles but they provide the most correct interpretation we have. The Bible is not simply good literature. The Bible is not to be interpreted by people as they see fit. "But know this first of all, that no prophecy of Scripture is a matter of one's own interpretation, for no prophecy was ever made by an act of human will, but men moved by the Holy Spirit spoke from God." (2 Peter 1:20-21).

The theme of the Bible is God's plan for the establishment of His kingdom. In essence, in order for God to establish His kingdom on earth, all sin and the influence of sin must be abolished and holiness and righteousness must be established. It begins with the original creation. At creation all things were made perfect and holy. There was no sin. There were no weeds to infest the garden. There were no storms to destroy the earth. There were no wild animals to attack and harm the people. There was no sorrow or sickness or pain. There was no death. But God created man in his image and gave him free will. He had the will to choose right from wrong. He had the ability to obey God or to disobey God. Satan deceived Eve in the

Garden of Eden. He told her that if she ate from the tree of knowledge of good and evil she would be like God. Eve believed Satan. She disobeyed God and ate the forbidden fruit even though she knew God had said not to eat of the tree in the middle of the garden. She then gave some of the fruit to her husband and he ate of it also. Thus both fell into sin. As a result, God banished them from the Garden of Eden and cut off their access to the tree of life. Furthermore, God cursed the serpent and caused him to crawl on his belly and eat the dust of the earth. He cursed the woman causing her to have great pain in childbirth. And He cursed Adam causing him to have to work by the sweat of his brow for a living. He cursed the ground and made thorns and thistles to grow in the midst of the crops. And finally, he condemned man to die. Since the fall man is no longer born in the image of God but is born in the image of fallen man. "When Adam lived 130 years, he became the father of a son in his own likeness, according to his image, and named him Seth." (Gen. 5:3). From Seth comes Noah and from Noah all future mankind. All people today are born, not in the image of God, but in the image of fallen Adam.

This is the state we find ourselves in today. We live in a fallen world. The whole earth is cursed. We have storms and natural disasters that destroy, we have sickness and disease that destroys life, we have weeds and thistles that infest our gardens, we have insects that bite and make us miserable and insects that destroy our crops, we have to work hard to make ends meet, we have hatred and discontent between our fellow man. We could go on and on with this. Aside from the fallen state of the world in which we live, man himself is corrupt. All are born in sin. "All have turned aside, together they have become useless; there is none who does good, there is not even one." (Rom. 3:12). Thus, we not only live in an alien world that is set against us, but our fellow man is in competition against us. Even those we call our friends often work against us when it suits their advantage. We are our own worst enemies. We accept and believe the secular lies of the world and drive ourselves to obtain as many of the great treasures as we can. We believe that this world was created for us and our own good pleasure and we expend the majority of our time, money and energy basking in worldly pleasures often at the expense of family, friends, and yes, even our relationship to God. There is no hope in this world if left to itself, but God has a plan which will upset all of creation.

In the end all evil will be destroyed. God will select for Himself a people to inhabit a New Heaven and a New Earth. Through the ages to come God will set apart those who are faithful to Him. Little by little His kingdom will increase until He has all those He desires. God will sanctify them. He will purify them. And He will make them holy. Likewise the earth and everything in it will be purified with fire. The old will pass away and a New Heaven and New Earth will emerge. This new creation will be without the old curse. There will be no more sorrow or pain. There will be no more storms, earthquakes, floods, and natural disasters that destroy. There will be no more weeds and thistles to infest our gardens or insects that bite us and bring sickness. There will be no more insects to destroy our crops. There will be no more infectious disease or death. All of nature will be at peace. The people will walk side by side with the wild animals. There will be no hate and discontent. There will be no sin. God Himself will walk among His people. He will be a Father to them and they will be His children.

During the time from the fall to the recreation, God is choosing for Himself a people to rule with Him in the final kingdom forever and ever. All are condemned by the fall. The seed of sinful Adam is passed down from generation to generation, even to today. However, God chooses some to be saved and in doing so, "He has made us to be a kingdom, priests to His God and Father." (Rev. 1:6). When God has completed His selection He will bring an end to the current order, where evil reigns, and set up a new order, where righteousness reigns.

How does He do this? All the earth must be purged of evil and the effects of evil. The current heavens and earth will be burned up with intense heat. Then New Heavens and a New Earth will emerge without the effects of sin. No more weeds, no more storms, no more gnats, no more wild animals (the wild animals have been tamed and will walk in peace among the people), all nature will be at peace with itself and with God's people. The curse on the earth will be removed.

Those whom God chooses to save will also be purged of all evil. They will be born again with a new spirit. They will be sanctified and they will be purified and they will be made holy. Each and every day God reveals to us something we need to change about ourselves. Our willingness to change and be changed is often followed by God's blessing. However, our unwillingness to change and be changed often results in God's discipline. God is continually refining and purifying us throughout our life. He is continually teaching us, testing us and preparing us for the day when we will meet Him face to face. We will never be perfect as long as we reside in this world. But when we are taken to heaven, we will be glorified and made perfect in every way. And God rejoices in being able to say to us, "Well done my good and faithful servant." (Matt. 25:21)

As we look at the Bible we can see there is a balance between the Old Testament and the New Testament:

Scripture begins with the creation of the world and it ends with the recreation of the world.

After the creation is the fall and sin is introduced. Immediately before the recreation is the purging of all sin.

After the fall is the flood. Before the purging of sin is the judgment

After the flood God chooses Abraham. Before the judgment God chooses all people

After the choosing of Abraham is the earthly kingdom of David. Before the choosing of all people is the heavenly kingdom of Jesus.

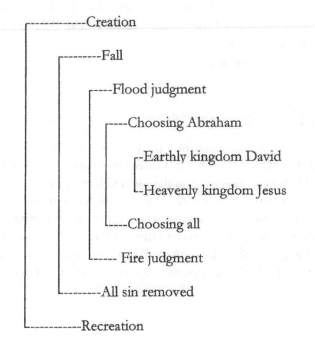

```
┌-----------Creation
│  ┌--------Fall
│  │  ┌----Flood judgment
│  │  │  ┌----Choosing Abraham
│  │  │  │  ┌-Earthly kingdom David
│  │  │  │  └-Heavenly kingdom Jesus
│  │  │  └----Choosing all
│  │  └----- Fire judgment
│  └--------All sin removed
└-----------Recreation
```

God's Word is an amazing and exciting story. We are intrigued by the creation story, comforted by the Psalms, puzzled by the Proverbs, awed with the Exodus, overwhelmed by the detailed history, amazed by the accuracy of the prophets, warmed by the gospels, and confused by the Revelation. Because the Revelation seems to confuse most people, most people avoid reading it. Yet it is the climax of the story. It is the reason for everything else. It is exciting. It is the final call to salvation. Jesus will come and gather His elect and we will ride with Him as He cleanses the earth of all evil people. We will reign with Christ on this earth for 1000 years during which time Satan will be bound. At the end of the 1000 years Satan will be released and make his last charge against the elect and be destroyed. Satan will be cast into the lake of fire. Those who dwell on earth will be judged and thrown into the lake of fire. All evil will be destroyed. A New Heaven and New Earth will be created. A New Jerusalem will come down from heaven. And we will live with God forever, and ever. In the New Heavens and New Earth there will be no more pain, no more suffering, no more weeds, no more hatred, envy or strife, no more tears. All things will be made new. The old will have passed away. We will walk the streets of gold with Adam, Noah, Abraham, Moses, Isaac, Jacob, David, all of the Old Testament faithful, all the apostles, Jesus, and all the New Testament faithful. All our brothers and sisters in Christ will be there. We will have finally come home. We Win!

THE FEASTS

God has revealed the story from the Exodus to the New Creation in the institution of the Feasts. God has instituted seven feasts to remind His people of the way He has cared for them in the past and how He will care for them in the future. Each feast is a reminder of past events that bring about temporary relief and at the same time point to a future event that will bring permanent relief. There are four spring feasts and three fall feasts. The four spring feasts lead up to the giving of the Law. The fall feasts end with the remembrance of God's care and protection during the 40 years in the wilderness.

Spring Feasts

The first feast is Passover.

The first Passover supper was eaten in preparation for the Exodus from Egypt. The Passover lamb was killed and the blood was put on the doorposts of the houses. During the Passover the angel of death came through Egypt killing all the first born of Egypt, he would pass over the households with the blood of the lamb on the doorposts. This feast is a reminder to the Jewish people that they were redeemed from slavery in Egypt and were headed towards the promised land of Canaan. Details of the event can be found in Exodus Chapter 12.

The feast of Passover points to the final day of redemption when Jesus gives Himself up to be the Passover Lamb for His people. Jesus eats a last meal with His disciples in about 33 AD. He is arrested, tried, and taken to Calvary. Jesus is crucified on a cross between two thieves. Jesus dies at 3 PM in the afternoon of the day of the Passover celebration. This is the exact time that the Passover lamb is slaughtered. This is the fulfillment of the feast of Passover. No other Passover lamb will ever need to be killed. Jesus is the final sacrifice. His death covers all the sins of the past, present, and future. Those who accept Jesus as their Lord and Savior are marked with His blood and are redeemed from slavery to sin and assured entry into the final Promised Land.

The second feast is the Feast of Unleavened Bread

This feast begins immediately after the Passover and lasts for seven days. All leaven is removed from the house and the Jewish people eat only unleavened bread during this feast. This is symbolic of the purging of sin that was introduced by the Egyptian way of life. It is detailed in Leviticus Chapter 23.

This feast is fulfilled during the period of time between the death of Jesus on the cross and His resurrection. Jesus during this time goes to Hades, defeats Satan, fully pays the penalty for sin for all times, and the penalty and guilt of sin is removed from all God's people for all times. This is the final purging of sin for God's people.

The third feast is the Feast of First Fruits.

This feast commemorates the day Israel ate of the first fruits of the harvest in the Promised Land after crossing the Red Sea. This signifies a new beginning for Israel.

This feast is fulfilled at the resurrection of Christ from the dead. Jesus is the First Fruit of the resurrection. "Now Christ has been raised from the dead, the first fruits of those who are asleep." (1 Cor.15:20). The resurrection of Christ from the dead marks the final new beginning for God's people.

The fourth feast is the Feast of Pentecost

This feast is celebrated to mark the giving of the Law at Mt Sinai. The giving of the Law took place 50 days after the Feast of First Fruits, thus the feast of Pentecost. All Jewish males were required to celebrate this feast at the temple in Jerusalem.

The Feast of Pentecost was fulfilled in the giving of the Holy Spirit on the day of Pentecost 50 days after the resurrection of Christ from the dead. The Holy Spirit wrote the Law of God on the hearts of His people.

This is the last of the spring feasts. The spring feasts have all had their final fulfillment. We are living in a time between the spring feasts and the fall feasts.

Fall Feasts

The fifth feast is the Feast of Trumpets

This feast commemorates the beginning of a new year. The Jewish people call this Rosh Hashanah which means "head of the year." It is a high holy day and is celebrated with rest, an offering made with fire, and the blowing of the trumpets.

This feast will be fulfilled in the future with the blowing of seven trumpets ending with the seventh trumpet when Christ returns to gather His elect. The final call to repentance begins with the sounding of the first trumpet. Many will accept Christ and be saved during the time of the trumpets. However, once the last trumpet is blown the call to repentance is over.

THE SIXTH FEAST IS THE DAY OF ATONEMENT

This feast is Yom Kippur. It is a holy convocation. The Lord called the people of Israel together in His presence to give complete undivided attention to Him. This is a time for fasting and repentance. This is a day for mourning over their sins. "If there is any person who will not humble himself on this day, he shall be cut off from his people." (Lev. 23:29). The Day of Atonement was a Sabbath day of rest and the Israelites were forbidden to do any work on this day, period. If they disobeyed they were liable to capital punishment. For details see Leviticus 16.

The Day of Atonement will be fulfilled with the blowing of the seventh trumpet when all God's elect will be taken up followed by the pouring out of God's wrath on all mankind.

THE SEVENTH FEAST IS THE FEAST OF BOOTHS.

This feast commemorates the period of time when Israel was in the wilderness for forty years. Israel was made to live in tents and rely entirely on God's provision during this time. God was present among them. He led them every step of the way and made certain they had food, water, and clothing. This feast signifies the temporary housing erected by Israel during the Exodus wanderings. The booths are symbolic of the protection, preservation, and shelter God provided during this time. Israel is being taught to rely entirely on God before they enter the Promised Land. At the onset of the feast God has directed, "Now, on the first day you shall take for yourselves the foliage of beautiful trees, palm branches and boughs of leafy trees and willows of the brook, and you shall rejoice before the LORD your God for seven days." (Lev. 23:40).

This final feast will find its fulfillment in the Millennium. The feast of Booths is a picture of the future kingdom of God. It will be a time of great rejoicing. It will be a time when we enter into glory with Christ and rule with Him. God will be in our midst and He will give us all things. It is a time in which God will prepare us to enter into the final new creation.

SUMMARY OF THE FEASTS

These seven feasts are a picture of how God plans to redeem His people. We are living in the end times, waiting for the trumpet to blow. We need not fix our hearts on the things of this world nor put our dependence on material things. What is today will be no longer. There will be difficult times ahead for God's people. There will be times of trials and tribulation. But we need not be discouraged. This time is short. Our focus is on the future. Christ is coming soon and He will establish His kingdom free of all sin and the effects of sin. There will be no more tears, no more pain, no more suffering, no more mourning, no more crying, for the first things will have passed away and we will reign with Him forever and ever.

Overview of the Revelation

The book of Revelation is not written in a pure chronological manner. Much of Revelation is sequential, however, in places John, who has recorded the Revelation of Jesus, inserts details, descriptions or broad overviews of events that have already taken place or are about to take place in order to give us a better understanding of Revelation.

The book of Revelation begins with an introduction in chapter 1. Chapters two and three are letters written to the seven churches in Asia. Even though much of Revelation follows one thing directly after another there is a huge gap in time between Chapter three and the rest of the book. Chapters 2 and 3 are current to John's day and the rest of Revelation is about events that take place sometime in the distant future. Even though the letters are written specifically to the church in John's day these letters also apply to the church today and to all future churches up until the removal of the church from the earth.

Chapters 4 through 11 are chronological and generally cover the seven seals and the seven trumpets.

Chapters 12 through 14 do not follow after chapter 11. They are inserted as additional detail of end time events. Chapter 12 gives a broad overview of events from the establishment of the nation of Israel up through the seventh trumpet. Chapter 13 gives some detailed information concerning the Antichrist and the False Prophet. Chapter 14 is an overview from the seventh trumpet up to the final battle.

Chapters 15 and 16 immediately follow the events of chapter 11 and cover the events of the seven bowls of wrath.

Chapter 17 covers the proclamation of the fall of Babylon.

Chapter 18 covers the fall of Babylon and happens sometime during the seven trumpets, most likely just before the seventh trumpet.

Chapter 19 concerns the coming of Jesus to gather His elect and His leading them on to victory at Armageddon. The first part of Chapter 19 immediately follows the seventh trumpet of Chapter 11 and the second part immediately follows the sixth bowl of wrath in Chapter 16.

Chapter 20 covers the thousand year reign of Christ on the present earth and the final battle. It follows the seventh bowl of wrath.

Chapters 21 and 22 cover the recreation of heaven and earth and they follow in sequence after Chapter 20.

We need to have a general understanding of how the book of Revelation is organized before we begin with the details. In the book of Revelation there is an introduction; four visions; and a conclusion. Each of the four visions is introduced by John saying, "I was in the spirit."

The first vision begins in Chapter 1 verse 9-11; "I, John, your brother and companion in the suffering and kingdom and patient endurance that are ours in Jesus, was on the island of Patmos because of the Word of God and the testimony of Jesus. On the Lord's Day I was in the spirit and I heard behind me a loud voice like a trumpet, which said: "Write on a scroll what you see and send it to the seven churches: to Ephesus, Smyrna, Pergamum, Thyatira, Sardis, Philadelphia, and Laodicea." The first vision will deal with the message John is to deliver to the seven churches. The first vision describes the state of the church in John's day as well as the current state of the church today.

The second vision begins in Chapter 4:1. "After this I looked, and there before me was a door standing open in heaven. And the voice I had first heard speaking to me like a trumpet said, 'Come up here, and I will show you what must take place after this.' At once I was in the Spirit, and there before me was a throne in heaven with someone sitting on it." The second vision takes place in heaven and will describe what must take place before we come to the end.

The third vision begins in Chapter 17:3. "And he carried me away in the Spirit into a wilderness; and I saw a woman sitting on a scarlet Beast, full of blasphemous names, having seven heads and ten horns." The third vision takes place in the wilderness and is concerned with the fall of Babylon. It describes what must take place on earth before we come to the end.

The fourth vision begins in Chapter 21:10. "And he carried me away in the Spirit to a great and high mountain, and he showed me the holy city, Jerusalem, coming down out of heaven from God." This vision describes the New Jerusalem and the New Heaven and New Earth.

Each of the visions is separate and distinct. Each vision stands by itself and does not depend on earlier visions for its support nor does it lend support to future visions. Each vision takes place in a different setting. The first vision takes place on the island of Patmos where John was imprisoned at the time he wrote the book of Revelation. The events of the first vision take place on the current earth. The second vision takes place in heaven and describes things that take place in heaven. The third vision takes place in the wilderness and describes things which take place in the wilderness. And the final vision takes place on a high mountain and describes the New Jerusalem coming down out of heaven and resting on the mountain.

Except for the introduction and final conclusion, all of the Revelation is contained within these four visions. The first vision is different from the other three in that it contains seven letters written to the seven churches of Asia. Each of the letters is written to a specific church, whereas the other three visions are written to the seven churches collectively and the church today. Also, the first vision speaks about the present state of the churches and the other three visions speak of future events to take place.

In addition to the four visions there are three signs in heaven: (1) "a woman clothed with the sun, and the moon under her feet, and on her head a crown of twelve stars." (2) "a great Red Dragon having seven heads and ten horns," (3) "Seven angels with seven plagues." These signs provide additional detail to the Revelation. They are a part of the second vision but are not placed chronologically within the vision. A sign is something that points to something else. For instance the rainbow is a sign which reminds us of the covenant that God made with the world that it would never be totally destroyed by water again. (Gen. 9:13) The Sabbath was given as a sign that God created all things in a matter of six days and on the seventh day He rested. (Ex. 31:17) Throughout the Bible there are many wonders and signs. The three signs in Revelation all paint a picture for us to show us some truth about God and His plan for us. The signs themselves are not to be literally interpreted but provide a graphic illustration of things to come or things that have already occurred.

We will approach our discussion of the book of Revelation through literal interpretation. Everything that can be interpreted literally will be so interpreted and those things which set themselves apart by their own interpretation as symbolic will be understood as symbolic. In other words, if something says it is symbolic it is symbolic; if it does not say it is symbolic, it is literal. We will encounter some things that are better understood if they are defined ahead of time. For instance, Jesus is referred to as "the Lion that is from the tribe of Judah", the "Root of David," a "Lamb", "a male child," and "One who is called Faithful and True." The church is identified as a "lampstand," "His army" and, "bride." The enemies of the church are identified as "the great Red Dragon," "Beast," "Beast of the Sea," "Beast of the Earth," and the "Great Harlot."

Now, as you prepare to study this exciting conclusion to the greatest masterpiece of all times, let your heart be open to hear God speak to you through His Word. Forget all you ever heard about the book of Revelation. Willingly accept it for what it is. It is God's clear plan for the future. God wants you to know what is about to happen. "Blessed is he who reads, and those who hear the Words of the prophecy and heed the things which are written in it; for the time is near." (Rev. 1:3) Reading the prophecy is not sufficient. To be blessed by God's Word we must hear what the Word says. This means that we must open our hearts to let His Holy Spirit teach us His Word. And finally, we must heed the Word of prophecy. In other words, we must take action on what we learn from God's Word.

We are cautioned to take this book very seriously and to read it for what it says. We are not to put foolish interpretation on it. "I testify to everyone who hears the Words of the prophecy of this book: if anyone adds to them, God will add to him the plagues which are written in this book; and if anyone takes away from the words of the book of this prophecy, God will take away his part from the tree of life and from the holy city, which are written in this book." (Rev. 22:18-19) And so, humbly, I present before you a literal view of the book of Revelation.

Your teacher for this and any study of God's Word is the Holy Spirit. Pray and seek His guidance as you study God's Word.

QUESTIONS OVERVIEW

1. Read the book of Revelation through at least two times. Read in the Spirit of literal interpretation. Read everything that can be interpreted literally as being literal.

2. Learn what you can about the seven Feasts. Leviticus 23

   a. Passover
   b. Unleavened Bread
   c. First Fruits
   d. Festival of Weeks (Pentecost)
   e. Feast of Trumpets
   f. Day of Atonement
   g. Feast of Tabernacles (Booths)

3. Each of the feasts celebrate an historical event, what is the event and when is it celebrated?

   a. Passover   Leviticus 23:4-5; Exodus 12:1-14

   b. Unleavened Bread   Leviticus 23:6-8; Exodus 12:33-34;
                            Exodus 12:12-20;
                            Exodus 13:6-8; Exodus 23:15:
                            Exodus 34:18;
                            Deuteronomy 16:3,8

   c. First Fruits   Leviticus 23:9-14;

   d. Festival of Weeks   Leviticus 23:15-21;
                            Deuteronomy 16:9

e. Feast of Trumpets   Leviticus 23:23-25;

f. Day of Atonement   Leviticus 23:26-32

g. Feast of Tabernacles   Leviticus 23:33-43;
                                     Exodus 23:16;
                                     Exodus 34:22; Nehemiah 8:13-18;
                                     Deuteronomy 16:14

4. Each of the feasts also point to a future event, what is the event?

a. Passover   John 19:14; 1 Peter 1:18-19;
                 John 1:29; 1 Corinthians 5:7

Compare Exodus 12:46 and John 19:31

b. Unleavened Bread   2 Corinthians 5:21;
                        1 Corinthians 5:7;
                        John 6:35

c. First Fruits   1 Corinthians 15:20, 23

d. Festival of Weeks   Acts 2:1-4

e. Feast of Trumpets   1 Thessalonians 4:13-18;
                      1 Corinthians 15:52

f. Day of Atonement   Zechariah 12:10
                     Romans 11:1-6, 25-36

g. Feast of Tabernacles   Micah 4:1-7

CHAPTER 1

Introduction to Revelation

*B*efore going on I would ask that you sit down, pray for the Holy Spirit to guide you, and read through the book of Revelation in the spirit of truth, seeking to believe it literally for what it says. Do this when you have time to read the book straight through in one sitting. Try to put aside and forget anything you have previously heard or studied about Revelation. Put aside any preconceived ideas about the book and simply "hear what the Spirit says to the churches."

Now you are ready. Read chapter 1 of Revelation.

"The Revelation of Jesus Christ, which God gave Him to show to His bond-servants, the things which must soon take place; and He sent and communicated it by His angel to His bond-servant John, who testified to the Word of God and to the testimony of Jesus Christ, even to all that he saw. Blessed is he who reads and those who hear the Words of the prophecy, and heed the things which are written in it; for the time is near." (Rev. 1:1-3).

John was not the author. The author was God who is absolute, accurate, true, faithful, trustworthy, and reliable. Jesus passed the revelation to John through His angel. Jesus also is absolute, accurate, true, faithful, trustworthy, and reliable. The revelation is communicated to John by the angel of Jesus who is also absolute, accurate, true, faithful, trustworthy, and reliable. In other words the book of Revelation is the holy, inspired, infallible, and inerrant Word of God.

John recorded the Book of Revelation. Who was John? John was a bondservant of Christ who bore witness to the Word of God, to the testimony of Jesus Christ, and to all he saw. He was a spiritual brother in Christ and fellow partaker or fellow participant with others in the tribulation, in the kingdom and in the perseverance in Christ. John was a follower of Christ Jesus. Because he followed Jesus he has faced many trials and tribulations. Yet he persevered. In spite of his hardships he remained faithful.

John was imprisoned as a common criminal at the time he wrote Revelation. He had been put in prison on the Isle of Patmos because he had refused to be silent concerning the gospel of Christ. As John sat in prison he was entrusted with the Revelation of Jesus which was given to Him by God in order that His bondservants might know the things which must soon take place. God wants the bondservants of Jesus to know what will take place in the end. The Revelation was not and is not intended to be some secret message impossible to decipher. Revelation was meant for believers of all times to know, understand, and believe. God sent the Revelation to John by His angel and John recorded it for us to read and understand. In Revelation 1:3 we are given a promise. "Blessed is he who reads and those who hear the words of the prophecy, and heed the things which are written in it, for the time is near." Reading the book of Revelation is not enough. We must hear the words of the prophecy. To hear the words means to accept and understand the words. "But know this first of all, that no prophecy of Scripture is a matter of one's own interpretation, for no prophecy was ever made by an act of human will, but men moved by the Holy Spirit spoke from God." (2 Peter 1:21-22). We must rely on the power of the Holy Spirit to enable us to hear the Word of prophecy. It is only by His Spirit that we are able to hear God's Word speak to us. But, even so, reading and hearing the prophecy is not enough. We must also heed the things written in it. Our blessing comes when we take seriously what God is speaking to us and allow His Word to change how we live our lives.

"John, to the seven churches that are in Asia: Grace to you and peace, from Him who is and who was and who is to come, and from the seven Spirits who are before His throne." (Rev. 1:4). The Revelation is written to the seven churches in Asia. These churches are described in more detail in chapters 2 and 3. However, although the Revelation was written specifically to these seven churches, it finds its fulfillment in the churches to come and thus is applicable to the church today as it awaits the second coming of Christ. The seven Spirits is a reference to the Holy Spirit that operates within the seven churches.

"and from Jesus Christ, the faithful witness, the firstborn of the dead, and the ruler of the kings of the earth. To Him who loves us and released us from our sins by His blood . . . " (Rev. 1:5). Jesus is the faithful witness, the firstborn of the dead, and the ruler of the kings of the earth. Jesus is the faithful witness of all creation. He was from the beginning, is and will be forever. Jesus is described as eternal. He is, He was, and He is to come. John is well aware of the eternal nature of Jesus. In his gospel John writes, speaking of Jesus, "In the beginning was the Word and the Word was with God and the Word was God. He was in the beginning with God. All things came into being through Him and apart from Him nothing came into being." (John 1:1-3). As Jesus was from the very beginning He has witnessed all things since the beginning. Nothing has escaped the scrutiny of His eye.

Jesus is the firstborn of the dead. He is the first to be bodily resurrected. He is proof positive of eternal life. Because He lives we can know for sure that we also will live.

Jesus is the ruler of the kings of the earth. All things on earth are subject to Him. He is Lord of lords and King of kings. "angels and authorities and powers had been subjected to Him." (1 Peter 3:22).

Jesus loved us and released us from our sins by His blood. Jesus loved us so much that He gave up His very life in order that we may live. He is the One and only sufficient sacrifice that takes away the sins of the world. Having been born in sin we are enslaved to sin. In our natural state we are ruled by sin and can do no good. However, when Jesus died on the cross He took with Him all the sins of the world and fully and completely paid the required penalty to absolve all those who believe in Him. There is no more blame, no more guilt, and no more responsibility for the sins of the believers. Jesus has released us from all of that. We are now freed from the power of sin, we are freed from the penalty of sin and we will one day be freed from the presence of sin. The book of Revelation is, in fact, about the cleansing of the world of sin and the effects of sin so that we will be able to live in a new creation freed from the presence of sin forever and ever. By the blood of Jesus we are freed from the power of sin, we are freed from the penalty of sin, and one day we will be freed from the presence of sin.

"He has made us to be a kingdom, priests to His God and Father, to Him be the glory and dominion forever and ever, Amen." (Rev. 1:6). All those who accept Christ as their Lord and Savior are made a part of the kingdom of God. There are two classifications of people on this earth. There are those who dwell on earth and those who dwell in heaven. That is, those who put their stock and faith in earthly things and those who put their stock and faith in heavenly things. There is the kingdom of Satan and the kingdom of God. We are born in sin and so we are naturally a part of the kingdom of Satan. But Christ has made those who believe in Him to be a part of the kingdom of God. God is our Father and we are His children. God looks after us, provides for us, cares for us, loves us and yes, disciplines us. We, as God's children, trust in God. We need not worry over the things of this world. "God causes all things to work out to good for those who love Him and are called according to His purpose." (Rom. 8:28). Furthermore we have a special place in the kingdom. We are priests to God the Father. We serve Him, we worship Him, and we are His image and His voice in the world. The office of priesthood is not to be taken lightly. It is the highest of honors. Those in the priesthood are chosen by God to serve Him. We represent God to the world. It is our priestly duty to proclaim the gospel to everyone we can.

"Behold, He is coming with the clouds, and every eye will see Him, even those who pierced Him; and all the tribes of the earth will mourn over Him. So it is to be, Amen. 'I am the Alpha and the Omega' says the Lord God, who is and who was and who is to come, the Almighty.", (Rev. 1:7-8). "The Lord Himself will descend from heaven with a shout, with the voice of the archangel and with the trumpet of God, and the dead in Christ will rise first, then those who are alive and remain will be caught up together with them in the clouds to meet the Lord in the air, and so we shall always be with the Lord." (1 Thess. 4:16-17). This is one of the greatest promises in Scripture. Christ Jesus will come back and gather together His elect from the four corners of the earth and they will live with Him forever and ever. No matter what this world has to offer we can know for sure that a time will come when we will be rescued from the trials and tribulations of this world and we will live in peace with all creation. Every eye will see Jesus when He returns: the righteous, the unrighteous, the living and the dead. Everyone will know that Jesus is Lord. It will be a time of great rejoicing for those who believe but for others it will be a time of sorrow and fear. Those in the kingdom will prepare to receive their reward. It will be too late for the rest, they will know they have made a dreadful mistake, and they will wait for the final judgment knowing there is no hope for their souls. Jesus is the Alpha and Omega, the beginning and the end. He is eternal God. There was none before Him and there will be none beyond Him. He is, He was, and He is to come. He is the Almighty!

"I, John, your brother and fellow partaker in the tribulation and kingdom and perseverance which are in Jesus, was on the island called Patmos because of the Word of God and the testimony of Jesus" (Rev. 1:9-11). John is on the Isle of Patmos. John had been imprisoned there because of his preaching of God's Word and his testimony about Jesus. John says he is a brother. Those who know Christ Jesus are brothers and sisters. We are all children of God. We have the same Father as Jesus and we are all equal heirs to the kingdom. John says he is a fellow partaker in the tribulation and the kingdom and the perseverance which are in Christ Jesus. John's speaking of the tribulation here is not the great tribulation; it is the tribulation that all Christians face living in a fallen world. Those who are partakers of the kingdom are living in an alien world. This world is not our world. Evil and sin are all around us. Every day we find sickness, storms, weeds, biting insects, draughts, floods, earthquakes, murder, strife, jealousy, hatred, and all the effects of a fallen world. We must persevere until Christ comes again to rescue us. We must not lose faith but truly lean on the promises of God knowing that our God reigns. No matter what this world has to offer, no matter what tribulations we face, our God will get us through and promises us a new world void of all evil and sin and the effects that they bring. Our steadfast hope and perseverance through the tribulations of this world will be rewarded with the peace, comfort, and joy of a new world void of the effects of a fallen world.

John's first vision

"I was in the Spirit on the Lord's Day, and I heard behind me a loud voice like the sound of a trumpet, saying, "Write in a book what you see, and send it to the seven churches: to Ephesus and to Smyrna and to Pergamum and to Thyatira, and to Sardis and to Philadelphia and to Laodicea." (Rev. 1:10). John is instructed to record this vision and to present it to the seven churches in Asia. The message is for the churches in John's day. It describes the state of the churches and gives instructions and warnings to them. These instructions and warnings apply equally to our churches today as we see our churches described in one or more of the churches in John's vision. This vision is not static, meant only for the seven churches in Asia, but rather, it is intended for all churches of all times until the blowing of the seventh trumpet.

"Then I turned to see the voice that was speaking with me. And having turned I saw seven golden lamp stands; and in the middle of the lamp stands I saw one like a son of man, clothed in a robe reaching to the feet, and girded across His chest with a golden sash. His head and His hair were white like white wool, like snow; and His eyes were like a flame of fire. His feet were like burnished bronze, when it has been made to glow in a furnace, and His voice was like the sound of many waters. In His right hand He held seven stars, and out of His mouth came a sharp two-edged sword; and His face was like the sun shining in its strength." (Rev. 1:12-16). John turns and sees Jesus standing among seven lamp stands. How is Jesus described? He is "one like a son of man", that is he had the appearance of human form, "clothed in a robe reaching to the feet, and girded across His chest with a golden sash. His head and His hair were white like wool, like snow; and His eyes were like a flame of fire. His feet were like burnished bronze, when it has been made to glow in a furnace, and His voice was like the sound of many waters. In His right hand He held seven stars, and out of His mouth came a sharp two edged sword; and His face was like the sun shining in its strength."

"When I saw Him, I fell at His feet like a dead man. And He placed His right hand on me, saying, "Do not be afraid; I am the first and the last, and the living One; and I was dead, and behold, I am alive forevermore, and I have the keys of death and of Hades. Therefore write the things which you have seen, and the things which are, and the things which will take place after these things." (Rev. 1:17-19). We know this is Jesus because He places His right hand on John and says, "Do not be afraid ; I am the first and the last, and the Living One; and I was dead, and behold, I am alive forevermore, and I have the keys of death and of Hades." This can be none other than Christ Jesus who was from the beginning with God, who was born in the flesh, who died without sin yet took all the sin of the world to the grave, who was resurrected, and who lives today. It is He who has the key to death and Hades, He determines life and death and He determines final destinations.

John is instructed by Jesus to "Write the things which you have seen, the things that are, and the things that will take place after these things." In other words John is to write down in great detail all that is revealed to him. He is to write what he saw when he was taken to heaven. He is to write about the state of the churches. And he is to write about the things that will take place in the end.

"As for the mystery of the seven stars which you saw in My right hand, and the seven golden lamp stands: the seven stars are the angels of the seven churches, and the seven lamp stands are the seven churches." (Rev. 1:20). And then at the end of chapter 1 Jesus explains the symbols in John's first vision. Again, the message is for the seven churches in Asia. However, seven is a number of completeness and the message is not just for the seven churches in Asia but is for all churches of all times as long as they remain on this earth. We are speaking here of the physical church. The true church is all true believers grouped together as one. But, what is being described here are individual bodies of believers that meet together to worship God. These bodies all have a guardian angel that looks after and cares for them. We can conclude from this that the churches today have angels that look after and care for them. And finally, the seven churches are described as lamp stands. A lamp stand is something on which to place a lamp. The church has the expressed task of taking the light of Jesus out into the world. Jesus is the true light. But Jesus gives us an awful responsibility saying, "You are the light of the world." (Matt. 5:14). We, as Christians, are the light of the world. We are the ones who bring the light of Jesus into the world. "Put your light on a lamp stand so it will give light to all in the house." (Matt. 5:16 NASB). "Let your light shine before men in such a way that they may see your good works and glorify your Father who is in heaven." (Matt. 5:16). Our light, the light of Jesus that we have within our hearts, is to shine in the world so intensely that the darkness of the world will be overcome by the light of Christ Jesus.

> "He was the Lamp that was burning and was shining . . . " (John 5:35). Jesus speaking of John says he is the light of Christ.

> "Then Jesus spoke to them saying, "I am the Light of the world."" (John 8:12). Jesus is identified as the Light.

> "Jesus says, "I have placed you as a light for the gentiles . . ."" (Acts 13:47). Jesus gave the church the mission to be the light of Christ in the world.

Before the message to the seven churches is given to John it is made clear that the seven churches are not simply a group of people meeting together as some club or organization. The church is a body of believers with the responsibility to be the light of Christ in a fallen and dark world. That was the mission of the church in John's day and that is the mission of the church today.

Questions Chapter 1

Introduction

Read through the book of Revelation in the spirit of truth. That is, read it as though everything you read means exactly what it says.

As you read through the book do you find things that simply are not possible if interpreted literally?

Record a few of the things that you notice that are not intended to be interpreted literally and why you believe that they are symbolic.

In just a few Words what is the book about?

CHAPTER I

Read Revelation chapter 1

1. Who is the author of the book?

2. To whom is the book written?

3. Who recorded the book of Revelation?

4. What do we know about the recorder?

5. What three things must we do to receive a blessing?

Read Revelation chapter 1: 4, 5

6. Who does John send his greetings from?

7. What or who do you think the seven spirits are? See Revelation 3:1, 4:5, 5:6

Read Revelation 1:20

8. What are the lamp stands?

9. What are the seven stars?

10. Reading chapter 1 What do you learn about Jesus?

11. What three things has John been told to write?

12. The book of Revelation contains four separate visions. Each vision begins with John being "in the spirit".

Record where each vision takes place and what the immediate scene of the vision is. In just a few Words describe what the vision is about.

Revelation 1:10

Revelation 4:2

Revelation 17:3

Revelation 21:10

CHAPTER 2

Message to the Churches

MESSAGE TO THE CHURCH AT EPHESUS

Read Revelation 2:1-7

"To the angel of the church in Ephesus write: the One who holds the seven stars (angels) in His right hand and the One who walks among the seven golden lamp stands (the churches) says this, I know your deeds and your toil and perseverance, and that you cannot tolerate evil men, and you put to the test those who call themselves apostles, and they are not, and you found them to be false; and you have perseverance and have endured for My name's sake, and have not grown weary." (Rev. 2:1-3). The church at Ephesus is working hard to keep the church, or at least the leaders in the church, true to their Christian faith. They put them to the test and if they fail they remove them. This apparently is not a casual, haphazard effort. With great perseverance the church works to maintain a strong body of true apostles. Yet, they are not without fault.

"But I have this against you, that you have left your first love. Therefore remember from where you have fallen, and repent and do the deeds you did at first; or else I am coming to you and will remove your lamp stand from its place." (Rev. 2:4-5). They no longer do the deeds they once did. It doesn't say what those deeds are but it would seem that the church is not serving Christ in the community. It is perhaps turned in upon itself. Jesus calls for them to change their ways and repent or He will remove their lamp stand from its place. The church cannot survive for the sole purpose of sustaining itself from within. It cannot be a church simply for the sake of its own members. The church is called to reach out and serve others with deeds of kindness and mercy. The church is called to spread the gospel of Christ throughout the community in which it exists. The church is a lamp stand. The only purpose of a lamp stand is to hold a lamp which gives off light. The light is the gospel of Christ. When the church fails to let its light shine in the community and be disciples for Christ, Jesus will remove their place from among His chosen people.

"Yet this you do have, that you hate the deeds of the Nicolaitans, which I also hate." (Rev. 2:6). However, they hate the deeds of the Nicolaitans, which Jesus also hates. The Nicolaitans were a form of antinomianism. That is, they believed in the mercy of God as grounds for salvation, but they also believed that once a person is saved they can do as they please. The Law of God is no longer binding. They held to the freedom of the flesh and sin, teaching that the deeds of the flesh have no effect upon the health of the soul and they have no relation to salvation. Therefore they could live their life anyway they want to without regard for the Law. Paul addresses this same issue in his letter to the church in Rome, "What then? Shall we sin because we are not under the law but under grace? May it never be." (Rom. 6:15). We are freed from the penalty of sin, yes, but we are new creatures and slaves to obedience. We are also freed from the power of sin so sin no longer has its binds on us. Therefore we have the ability to turn away from sin. The church at Ephesus hated the doctrine of the Nicolaitans and held to a commitment of righteous living. Jesus gives them praise for this.

"He who has an ear, let him hear what the spirit says to the churches. To him who overcomes, I will grant to eat of the tree of life which is in the Paradise of God." (Rev. 2:7). Jesus promises that those who overcome the ways of the world and repent of their unfaithful behavior will be given eternal life. For the church in Ephesus, this means to remember their first love and spread the gospel of Christ throughout their community, doing deeds of mercy and kindness.

Today, there are churches which are self serving and have no concern for their neighbors. They exist for their own pleasure. They may, in fact, hold to the truth of Scripture concerning their desire to be righteous but they do not see the importance of reaching out into the community and being disciples for Christ. They hang a sign out front and have the attitude that if someone wishes to come, okay; if not, okay. They have no real interest in proclaiming the gospel in their community. Their light may shine in their righteous behavior but not in their love of their neighbor. They welcome those who come but they seek none. The message to the church at Ephesus is the message to this church today.

MESSAGE TO THE CHURCH AT SMYRNA

Read Revelation 2: 8-11

Jesus identifies Himself as the first and last, and the one who died and was resurrected. The church at Smyrna is apparently going under trials and tribulation for the gospel of Christ. Jesus says, "And to the angel of the church in Smyrna write: the first and the last, who was dead, and has come to life, says this, "I know your tribulation and your poverty (but you are rich), and the blasphemy by those who say they are Jews and are not, but are a synagogue of Satan.""" (Rev. 2:8-9). Jesus knows the difficulties this church is facing. The Jewish community where they reside is attacking them with verbal accusations. They are in financial poverty, possibly from having been shut out from the community. But Jesus says they are spiritually rich in their faith and perseverance.

"Do not fear what you are about to suffer. Behold, the Devil is about to cast some of you into prison, so that you will be tested, and you will have tribulation for ten days." (Rev. 2:9-10a). Things are bad now but it is going to get worse. Jesus tells them not to be afraid. He is with them. He knows what they are about to face and He will see them through it. The Devil is about to cast some of them in prison for testing and they will have tribulation for ten days. Jesus is giving the church at Smyrna confidence and comfort. Yes, things are hard now but hang in there. He has a great reward for them.

"Be faithful until death, and I will give you the crown of life. He who has an ear, let him hear what the Spirit says to the churches." (Rev. 2:10b-11a). Jesus tells them to remain faithful even unto death and He will give them the crown of life. Some of them will be martyred because of their faith. Jesus introduced Himself as having died and having been resurrected. This shows the church at Smyrna that there is life after death. And He concludes His message saying that, just as He was resurrected, they too, if they persevere, will also be resurrected to new life.

The church at Smyrna is left with a promise. "He who overcomes will not be hurt by the second death." (Rev. 2:11b). At the end of time there will be judgment. Those who remain faithful will inherit the New Heaven and New Earth. Those who reject Jesus will be thrown into the lake of fire. This is the second death. "Then death and Hades were thrown into the lake of fire. This is the second death, the lake of fire." (Rev. 20:14).

Jesus finds no fault with the church at Smyrna. He writes to them to assure them that even in these tough times God is alive and well and they will one day reign with Him.

"He who has an ear let him hear what the Spirit says to the churches." The church is under persecution in many parts of the world. They risk their lives every day just to assemble together in praise and worship of God. As we near the end of times there will be an increase in the persecution of the church. Jesus wants those who are in tribulation and poverty, because of their faith, to hold fast and persevere. God has not forgotten them.

MESSAGE TO THE CHURCH AT PERGAMUM

Read Revelation 2:12-17

"And to the angel of the church in Pergamum write: The One who has the sharp two-edged sword says this: 'I know where you dwell, where Satan's throne is; and you hold fast My name, and did not deny My faith even in the days of Antipas, My witness, My faithful one, who was killed among you, where Satan dwells." (Rev. 2:12-13). To the church at Pergamum Jesus describes Himself as the one with the two edged sword. In Hebrews the two edged sword is defined as the Word of God. "For the Word of God is living and active and sharper than any two edged sword, and piercing as far as the division of soul and spirit, of both joints and marrow, and able to judge the thoughts and intentions of the heart." (Heb. 4:12). We don't know anything about Antipas but he is described as a martyr in Pergamum. He had unrelenting faith and refused to deny his faith even unto death. Those in Pergamum continue to worship God and tell others about the saving grace of Christ Jesus even when they have seen Antipas martyred and they themselves are faced with persecution and possible death.

"But I have a few things against you, because you have there some who hold the teaching of Balaam, who kept teaching Balak to put a stumbling block before the sons of Israel, to eat things sacrificed to idols and to commit acts of immorality. So you also have some who in the same way hold the teaching of the Nicolaitans. Therefore repent; or else I am coming to you quickly, and I will make war against them with the sword of My mouth." (Rev. 2:14-16). Even though there are those in Pergamum who hold fast to their faith even unto death, these very ones allow others among them who hold to the teaching of Balaam and Balak and put stumbling blocks before the sons of Israel by eating things sacrificed to idols and committing acts of immorality. And there are some who hold to the teaching of the Nicolaitans. Balak summoned Balaam, a prophet, offering him a large sum of money to curse Israel. Balaam agreed to compromise his authority as a prophet but God caused him to bless Israel instead. Balak and Balaam were known to plot against Israel, causing them to trespass against the LORD. "Behold, these (Midianites) caused the sons of Israel, through the counsel of Balaam, to trespass against the LORD in the matter of Peor." (Num. 31:16). The church at Pergamum is exercising its freedom from the Jewish Law, leading others in their midst to do the same, causing them to sin. Eating of the food sacrificed to idols is not sinful for those whose faith is strong. However, for those who believe they must hold to the Law, it is sin. Jesus rebukes them for leading others astray by their selfish and arrogant ways.

"I am coming to you quickly, and I will make war against them with the sword of My mouth. He who has an ear let him hear what the Spirit says to the churches. To him who overcomes, to him I will give some of the hidden manna, and I will give him a white stone, and a new name written on the stone which no one knows but he who receives it." (Rev. 2:17). Jesus calls them to repent and will condemn those who fail to be compassionate and patient with those of the weaker faith. Jesus promises those who overcome in Pergamum that he will give them hidden manna, the food of eternal life, and they will get a new name written on a white stone. Those who maintain their faith through the trials and tribulations of this earth will have eternal life and their old name, tarnished with the sin of this world, will be replaced with a new name written on a clean slate, white as snow with no blemish.

There are churches today that are very faithful to the Word. Yet they have some among them who are arrogant and conceited, thinking they are better than the weaker brother. Their arrogance leads the weaker to destruction. They lack compassion and understanding. Their self centeredness will lead to their destruction unless they repent and show compassion and tolerance towards their weaker brother.

MESSAGE TO THE CHURCH AT THYATIRA

Read Revelation 2:18-28

"And to the angel of the church in Thyatira write: The Son of God, who has eyes like a flame of fire, and His feet are like burnished bronze, says this:" (Rev. 2:18). Jesus is described as having eyes like flaming fire. He sees all and His eyes are able to penetrate to the depth of the soul knowing not just the outward actions but the inward workings of the heart. His feet are like burnished bronze. He is steadfast, strong and unmovable.

Jesus says, "I know your deeds, and your love and faith and service and perseverance, and that your deeds of late are greater than at first." (Rev. 2:19). The church at Thyatira is a working church. They have a great love for God and their fellow man. They do deeds of service, perhaps helping the poor, taking care of the widow, mending the houses of the elderly, and generally caring for those in the community showing God's love through service to others. And they persevere through their work even when it is difficult. Their deeds are increasing every day.

Yet, Jesus says, "But I have this against you, that you tolerate the woman Jezebel, who calls herself a prophetess, and she teaches and leads My bond-servants astray so that they commit acts of immorality and eat things sacrificed to idols. I gave her time to repent, and she does not want to repent of her immorality. Behold, I will throw her on a bed of sickness, and those who commit adultery with her into great tribulation, unless they repent of her deeds." (Rev. 2:20-22). Jezebel is teaching and leading the people in the church in unsound doctrine. She is tickling the ears of the people, telling them what they want to hear rather them holding them to the teaching of Scripture. "For a time will come when they will not endure sound doctrine; but wanting to have their ears tickled, they will accumulate for themselves teachers in accordance to their own desires." (2 Tim. 4:3). The church at Thyatira has allowed one to come into their midst and teach doctrine contrary to Scripture, allowing for any and all kinds of immorality.

Jesus says, "And I will kill her children with death; and all the churches shall know that I am He that searcheth the minds and hearts: and I will give unto each one of you according to your works." (Rev. 2:23). Those who hold to and accept the teachings of Jezebel will not survive the judgment. They will be judged by the flaming eyes of Jesus who penetrates the minds and hearts. They will be condemned to death.

Jesus continues, "But I say to you, the rest who are in Thyatira, who do not hold this teaching, who have not known the deep things of Satan, as they call them—I place no other burden on you. Nevertheless what you have, hold fast until I come. He who overcomes, and he who keeps My deeds until the end, TO HIM I WILL GIVE AUTHORITY OVER THE NATIONS; AND HE SHALL RULE THEM WITH A ROD OF IRON, AS THE VESSELS OF THE POTTER ARE BROKEN TO PIECES, as I also have received authority from My Father; and I will give him the morning star." (Rev. 2:24-28). Those who do not hold to the teachings of Jezebel are instructed to hold fast to what they know until Jesus returns. In the end those who overcome the evil of this world will be given authority over all nations and will rule them with a rod of iron as the vessels of the potter are broken to pieces. In the end Jesus will come against all the nations with a rod of iron. All the saints who persevere through this earthly time and remain faithful will come with Him. And the saints will destroy them like broken pieces of pottery when smashed with an iron rod. And the final reward of the saints is that they will be given the morning star, living with Jesus forever and ever.

"He who has an ear let him hear what the Spirit says to the churches." (Rev. 2:29). Today we may identify this church with one that is very mission oriented, works hard in the community, loves their neighbor, shows kindness wherever they can, yet refuses to accept the importance of sound doctrine. The church has no hard and fast doctrinal standards. They think one can believe whatever they want as long as they love others and do good to all. For them works are more important than doctrine.

CHAPTER 3

Message to the Churches Continues

MESSAGE TO THE CHURCH AT SARDIS

Read Revelation 3:1-6

"To the angel of the church in Sardis write: He who has the seven Spirits of God and the seven stars, says this: "I know your deeds, that you have a name that you are alive, but you are dead." (Rev. 3:1). Jesus is identified as the One who has the seven Spirits of God and the seven stars. The seven Spirits of God is the Holy Spirit that resides within the seven churches and the seven stars are the seven angels of the seven churches. The community sees this church. They appear active. They meet on a regular basis. They do work in the community. From all outward appearances they seem to be an active, vibrant church. But they are dead. The Holy Spirit is not active in the church. Most of the members are not born again Christians.

"Wake up, and strengthen the things that remain, which were about to die; for I have not found your deeds completed in the sight of My God. So remember what you have received and heard; and keep it, and repent. Therefore if you do not wake up, I will come like a thief, and you will not know at what hour I will come to you." (Rev. 3:2-3). Jesus calls the church to repent, to turn away from its worldly ways and turn to Christ. He says they have deeds but they are not completed in the sight of God. Worldly deeds, feeding the hungry, taking care of the weak and sick, providing for the poor are all good and noble deeds, but they are not complete unless they include spiritual feeding and restoration. Jesus says the church is spiritually dead.

"But you have a few people in Sardis who have not soiled their garments; and they will walk with Me in white, for they are worthy. He who overcomes will thus be clothed in white garments; and I will not erase his name from the book of life, and I will confess his name before My Father and before His angels." (Rev. 3:4-5). There are some in Sardis who have not soiled their garments. All have sinned and fall short of the glory of God. All have soiled their garments. The garments remain soiled unless they are washed. When one accepts Christ their garments are washed in the blood of Jesus. Having their garments washed they are as though they have never been soiled. These will walk with Jesus in the end, for they are worthy. His promise to the church is that those who overcome will be clothed in white and their names will not be erased from the book of life. He will confess their names before the Father and before His angels.

"He who has an ear, let him hear what the Spirit says to the churches." (Rev. 3:6). Many churches today are alive on the outside. They appear to be active vibrant churches. But they are little more than social clubs. For the most part the members are not committed Christians. They go to church because they were brought up to believe that going to church is the right thing to do. Or they go to church because they have friends who go to the church. They have not committed their lives to Christ and so they cannot take the Word of Christ out into the world. The church needs a spiritual revival. Unless they turn to Christ they will die.

MESSAGE TO THE CHURCH AT PHILADELPHIA

Read Revelation 3:7-13

"And to the angel of the church in Philadelphia write: He who is holy, who is true, who has the key of David, who opens and no one will shut, and who shuts and no one opens, says this: I know your deeds. Behold, I have put before you an open door which no one can shut, because you have a little power, and have kept My Word, and have not denied My name." (Rev. 3:7-8). Jesus introduces Himself as the One "who is holy, who is true, who has the key of David, who opens and no one can shut, and who shuts and no one opens." (Rev. 3:1-7). Jesus is holy and true. What He says we can believe and trust. He has the key to the city of David, Jerusalem. Jesus opens the door to the New Jerusalem to those He chooses. No one can close the door or stop them from entering. Jesus also closes the door to those He chooses and if He closes the door no one can open it. Those at the church at Philadelphia have been true to the Word of God and have not denied Jesus. There is but one way to eternal life and that is belief in the name of our Lord Jesus Christ.

"I know your deeds. Behold, I have put before you an open door which no one can shut, because you have a little power, and have kept My Word, and have not denied My name. Behold, I will cause those of the synagogue of Satan, who say that they are Jews and are not, but lie—I will make them come and bow down at your feet, and make them know that I have loved you." Rev. 3:8-9). Because of their faith and the way they have exercised their faith in their deeds Jesus gives them the assurance that they will enter into His kingdom and no one can prevent it; even those Jews in the synagogue who try to dissuade them. These Jews will one day recognize the error of their ways but it will be too late for them

"Because you have kept the Word of My perseverance, I also will keep you from the hour of testing, that hour which is about to come upon the whole world, to test those who dwell on the earth. I am coming quickly; hold fast what you have, so that no one will take your crown. He who overcomes, I will make him a pillar in the temple of My God, and he will not go out from it anymore; and I will write on him the name of My God, and the name of the city of My God, the New Jerusalem, which comes down out of heaven from My God, and My new name." (Rev. 3:10-12). Jesus further promises that He will keep them from the hour of testing which is about to come upon the whole world to test those who dwell on earth. This does not mean that they will not face trials and tribulations in this world. It means that they will not take part in the wrath of God to come. Those who keep the Word of Jesus and persevere through the temptations of this life will be awarded a crown in the life to come. He who overcomes, Jesus will "make a pillar in the temple of God and he will not go out from it anymore; and Jesus will write on him the name of God and the city of God, the New Jerusalem which comes down out of heaven from God, and the name of Jesus." There will be no confusing them.

They belong to God, they have free access to the New Jerusalem and they proudly display the name of Jesus.

"To him who has ears let him hear what the Spirit says to the churches." (Rev. 3:13). Jesus finds no fault in the church at Philadelphia. Churches today who hold fast the Word of God, proclaim the gospel of Christ and do not allow apostasy to creep in are like the church at Philadelphia. They are assured that they will have a place in the kingdom of God and they will enter into the New Jerusalem.

MESSAGE TO THE CHURCH AT LAODICEA

Read Revelation 3: 14-22

"To the angel of the church in Laodicea write: The Amen, the faithful and true Witness, the Beginning of the creation of God, says this:" (Rev. 3:14). Jesus is identified as the Amen, the faithful and true Witness, and the Beginning of the creation of God. Jesus is the Amen. He is all there is. There need not be anything else. Amen, it is done, it is over. He is the faithful and true Witness. He lived on the earth a perfect and holy life. He defeated Satan and proved that we too can defeat the power of Satan and overcome the temptations of this life. He died, went to hell, and was resurrected from the dead. He is proof positive of eternal life. He was from the beginning. The gospel of John begins, "In the beginning was to Word and the Word was with God and the Word was God." He was from the very beginning, He is now, and He always will be.

"I know your deeds, that you are neither cold nor hot. So because you are lukewarm, and neither hot nor cold, I will spit you out of My mouth." (Rev. 3:15-16). The church at Laodicea has no passion. They have no feeling. They simply go through the motions of worship. They believe because they are rich and need nothing that they can exist as an island unto themselves. They have no need to evangelize. Come if you want or don't come. It makes no difference to them. Because of this, Jesus says He will reject them.

"Because you say, "I am rich, and have become wealthy, and have need of nothing," and you do not know that you are wretched and miserable and poor and blind and naked, I advise you to buy from Me gold refined by fire so that you may become rich, and white garments so that you may clothe yourself, and that the shame of your nakedness will not be revealed;

and eye salve to anoint your eyes so that you may see." (Rev. 3:17-18). Jesus says they are spiritually wretched, and miserable, and poor, and blind, and naked. They are spiritually defunct. They are incapable of seeing what is going on around them. They are naked, their sins are completely exposed. They do not wear the white robe that Jesus provides that covers their nakedness. Jesus wants them to turn from their ways. He can and will provide for them the true riches of abundant life, He will cover their nakedness with white robes, and He will anoint their eyes so they can see the errors of their ways and see the path that leads to righteousness if they will turn to Him.

Jesus says, "Those whom I love, I reprove and discipline; therefore be zealous and repent. Behold, I stand at the door and knock; if anyone hears My voice and opens the door, I will come to him and dine with him and he with Me." (Rev. 3:19-20). There are consequences to wrong living. Jesus calls them to repentance. He does not want their lazy unemotional repentance. He wants them to be zealous in their repentance. He wants them to be excited knowing what lies ahead. Jesus is knocking on the door. He is waiting for an answer. He pleads with them to open the door so He can come in and be an integral part of their lives.

"He who overcomes, I will grant to him to sit down with Me on My throne, as I also overcame and sat down with My Father on His throne. He who has an ear let him hear what the Spirit says to the churches." (Rev. 3:21-22). Jesus promises that those who overcome will sit down with Him on His throne as He also overcame and sat down with His Father on His throne. Today there are churches that are turned completely in on themselves. They are self satisfied and self serving. They go through the motions of worship but are not worshipful. They sing songs of praise but are not in the attitude of praise. They are spiritually dead. They need a revival. They need to be revitalized, lifted up, set on fire, and reenergized. The real problem is that the focus of the church is on the church and the sustaining of the church rather than the focus being on the gospel of Christ.

He who has ears, let him hear what the Spirit says to the churches. The message to the seven churches is the message to the church today and for all times. Each church can evaluate themselves in light of the messages Jesus gives us here. They can see where they fall short of what Jesus expects and what they must do to repent. Any one church may not find its complement in one of the particular churches of Asia, but they can find their traits somewhere in the compilation of the seven churches. The bottom line is, the church can overcome. Whatever fault there is in the church, the church can repent and will be assured their place in the New Jerusalem. Just as this is a message to the churches, we might also recognize this as a message to the individual Christian. After all, the church is the body of believers. Each believer, as he reads the message to the church can place himself in the place of the church and evaluate his own spiritual life in light of what Jesus requires. What He requires and expects of the church collectively He requires and expects of the believer individually.

John's first vision is a vision of the current state of the church. It was the state of the church in 90AD and it is the state of the church today. In almost 2000 years nothing has changed. The kingdom of God is not established through incorporating the physical church as a whole into the kingdom. All within the physical church are not worthy of the kingdom. The final state of the church will be comprised of the universal body of true believers. These are the ones who overcome the apostasy of the church.

Identified within the seven churches we find:

> Those whose love has grown cold. They lack tolerance for the weaker brother. They are self righteous and judgmental. They are more interested in keeping their body of believers pure than they are in showing love and compassion to those outside their circle.

> Those who allow false doctrines. They have a liberal view of Scripture and tolerate any and all interpretations. They say it is okay for you to believe whatever you want as long as you base it on an interpretation of Scripture that satisfies your own understanding. They believe that there is no right interpretation, no one really knows the truth.

> Those who lead others astray. Their doctrine may be sound but in their zeal to freely exercise their freedom from the Law they encourage the weaker brothers to fall prey to sin. Total freedom from the Law only comes when the Law has become imbedded in the heart and the mind has no

awareness of it. To encourage those who do not have the Law embedded in their hearts to exercise their freedom from the Law and do as they desire causes them to fall into sin. Their heart's desire is still under Satan's control.

Those whose deeds are not worthy. The only worthy deeds are those which lift up and glorify God. We often think that those who build hospitals with their names on them or those who promote great charity programs in their names for the poor or disabled and the like are doing great and wonderful deeds. Yes, these deeds do benefit society, but if they are not done to the glory of God, they are not good deeds and they will not be remembered in the kingdom of God. Only those deeds which lift up and glorify God are worthy to be called good deeds. Churches are often guilty of taking the glory from God for the things they do. When a church claims that they have fed the hungry, given clothing to the poor, saved souls, raised money for a new life center, or done anything at all without giving all the credit and glory to God they have done no deed worthy of the kingdom. Jesus explicitly says, do not let anyone know your good deeds, your Father in Heaven knows.

Those who have no passion. They exist as a church for the sole purpose of their existence. They meet, they sing songs, they pray, they go through all the motions of worship but they have no zeal and passion for the Lord. They are lukewarm. They are not hot and on fire for the Lord. They do not greet each other and their visitors with exuberance, proclaiming boldly the love and mercy of God. And they are cold and reserved, maintaining a safe distance from others. They keep their love of God and the mercy and grace He has shown towards them personal and private. Rather, there is a coolness in meeting them. They are friendly but cautious. They keep their light under a bushel basket so no one will see it.

What does this say to you and me individually? Are we self righteous, looking and finding faults in our brother? Do we accept every doctrine that comes along because we have not studied God's Word enough to know the difference? Do we arrogantly boast of our freedom from the Law and encourage others to put aside their pious behavior? Do we give freely of our time, money and talents and make sure that we get proper credit for our good deeds? Are we apathetic about God the Father, God the Son and God the Holy Spirit, not wanting anyone to know who we are and what we believe? Jesus calls for us to repent and He offers an abundant eternal life for those who overcome.

QUESTIONS CHAPTER 2 & 3

The Seven Churches

Read through Revelation chapters 2 and 3. For each church write down the good things that are pointed out about the church in one column and write down the bad things about the church in a parallel column. Also write down what those who overcome will receive in a third column.

1. Where are the churches located?

What do we know about the following?

1. Nicolatians

   From this passage

   From other Scripture

   From other sources

   Why are the practices of the Nicolatians hated?

2. Antipas

   From this passage

   From other Scripture

   From other sources

   What are the "Days of Antipas?"

3. Balaam

   From this passage

   From other Scripture; Numbers 25, 2Peter 2:15, Jude 11, Micah 6:5

   From other sources

4. Balak

   From this passage

   From other Scripture; Numbers 22:2, 4; Josh 24:9

From other sources

5. Jezebel

   From this passage

   From other Scripture; 1Kings 16:31, 21:1-29

   From other sources

6. How is Jesus described?

7. What are the seven stars?

8. What are the seven golden lamp stands?

9. What are the seven spirits?

10. Exactly what is it we are to overcome?

11. What is John's first vision about?

Chapter 4

Scene in Heaven

Read Revelation Chapter 4

"*A*fter these things I looked, and behold, a door standing open in heaven, and the first voice which I had heard, like the sound of a trumpet speaking with me, said, "Come up here, and I will show you what must take place after these things"" (Rev 4:1). John's second vision concerns things which must take place before the end. In the letters to the churches John is seeing the church in the present. Now John looks beyond the present to things which will take place in the future. John is in the spirit and is taken up to heaven. This vision therefore is from a heavenly perspective. We will see all the events that must take place before God can recreate this world void of all evil, sin and the effects of sin. We have seen the state that the current church is in. Beginning with chapter 21 in Revelation we will see the final state of the church. God's people must be gathered together and all evil must be destroyed in order to transition from the current state of the church to the future state of the church.

Revelation chapters 4-16 describe what will take place as seen from heaven. Chapters 17 through 18 describe how this affects the earth. Set aside some time and read through chapters 4-16. Keep in mind what John is going to show you. Put aside any preconceived ideas. Pray that the Holy Spirit will give you understanding as you read. And finally believe what you read to be literally true.

31

These are the events of the second vision:

Chapter 4   John's arrival in heaven and his vision of the throne

Chapter 5   Finding one worthy to open the book and break the seals

Chapter 6   Opening the first six seals
Rider on the white horse
Rider on the red horse
Rider on the black horse
Rider on the ashen horse
Martyrs beneath the altar
Terror

Chapter 7   Interlude
Angels hold back the four winds
144,000 sealed
Great multitude at the throne

Chapter 8   Seventh seal opened
Prayers of the saints went up before God
Four angels blow their trumpets
Woe, woe, woe for the last three trumpets

Chapter 9   Fifth trumpet bottomless pit opened
Locusts invade the earth
First woe is past
Sixth trumpet army from the east
Four angels released and kill 1/3 of mankind
Second woe is past

Chapter 10   John eats the little book

Chapter 11   Two witnesses
Seventh trumpet

Chapter 12   Woman Israel
Red Dragon, Satan
Male Child, Jesus
War in heaven

Chapter 13   Beast from the Sea
             Beast from the Earth

Chapter 14   Mt Zion and the Lamb
             First angel preaches the gospel
             Second angel announces the fall of Babylon
             Third angel proclaims judgment on those who
             worship the Beast
             Reaping the harvest

Chapter 15   Seven bowls of wrath given to seven angels

Chapter 16   Six bowls of wrath poured out
             Armageddon
             Seventh bowl of wrath
             It is done

John's Second Vision

The events of John's second vision are sequential. There are seven seals, seven trumpets, and seven bowls of wrath. This vision encompasses everything that must take place before the end. Chapters 17 and 18 are details of the fall of Babylon announced in chapter 14. Chapters 19 and 20 give details concerning the time from the seventh trumpet until "It is done."

/Seven seals / Seven trumpets / Six bowls Armageddon / Seventh bowl / It is done /

(See full time line in the appendix)

Before continuing take a few minutes and read chapter 4 of Revelation.

"Immediately I was in the Spirit; and behold, a throne was standing in heaven, and One sitting on the throne. And He who was sitting was like a jasper stone and a sardius in appearance; and there was a rainbow around the throne, like an emerald in appearance. Around the throne were twenty-four thrones; and upon the thrones I saw twenty-four elders sitting, clothed in white garments, and golden crowns on their heads. Out from the throne come flashes of lightning and sounds and peals of thunder. And there were seven lamps of fire burning before the throne, which are the seven Spirits of God; and before the throne there was something like a sea of glass, like crystal; and in the center and around the throne, four living creatures full of eyes in front and behind. The first creature was like a lion, and the second creature like a calf, and the third creature had a face like that of a man, and the fourth creature was like a flying eagle. And the four living creatures, each one of them having six wings, are full of eyes around and within; and day and night they do not cease to say, "HOLY, HOLY, HOLY is THE LORD GOD, THE ALMIGHTY, WHO WAS AND WHO IS AND WHO IS TO COME."" (Rev. 4:2-8).

John finds himself before the throne of God when he is carried to heaven. Around the throne are twenty four elders, seven lamps of fire, and four living creatures all worshipping and praising God. God is worthy to receive glory and honor and power because He created all things, and because of His will they existed and were created. Their song of praise is, "Holy, holy, holy is the Lord God, the Almighty, who was, and who is, and who is to come." There has never been a time and there will never be a time when God is not. He is always and forever present.

Around the throne are 24 thrones and upon the thrones are 24 elders. Who are the twenty four elders?

> Jesus is speaking to the 12 disciples, "Truly I say to you, that you who have followed Me, in the regeneration when the Son of Man will sit on His glorious throne, you also shall sit upon twelve thrones, judging the twelve tribes of Israel." (Matt. 19:28).

> Luke also records this event. Jesus speaking to the twelve disciples, "You are those who have stood by Me in my trials; and just as My father has granted Me a kingdom, I grant you that you may eat and drink at My table in My kingdom, and you will sit on thrones judging the twelve tribes of Israel." (Lk. 22:30).

Twelve of the elders are the twelve disciples.

"I was glad when they said to me, "Let us go to the house of the LORD," "For there thrones were set for judgment, the thrones of the house of David." (Ps. 122:1, 5). The thrones are described as belonging to the house of David or the twelve tribes of Israel.

The other twelve elders are the twelve sons of Israel

The final kingdom will be ruled by twenty four elders. These twenty four were chosen by God to lead His people while on earth and they will resume their role in the new creation.

The twenty four elders are described as being clothed in white and having golden crowns on their heads.

Why are they clothed in white?

"But you have a few people in Sardis who have not soiled their garments; and they will walk with Me in white, for they are worthy." (Rev. 3:4).

To the church at Laodicea, "I advise you to buy from Me gold refined by fire so that you may become rich, and white garments so that you may clothe yourself, and that your shame and nakedness will not be revealed" (Rev. 3:18). Those with white garments will be able to walk with God for their sin and shame is covered and they will be declared worthy.

"And He was transfigured before them; . . . . and His garments became white as light." (Matt. 17:1, 2). White garments show the complete holiness and righteousness of Christ.

The white garments of the elders, and we will see later, all of the saints show that they have been purified and made holy and righteous. Those who accept Christ as their Lord and Savior will be washed in the blood of Christ, their sins will be covered completely, God will not see, nor remember, what they once were, they will have become new creatures born of God and the Spirit. They will have been made holy and righteous before God, and will therefore be able to come into His presence and dwell with Him.

Why do they have golden crowns on their heads?

"And He has made us to be a kingdom, priests to His God and Father." (Rev. 1:6). You might read all of verses 4-7 to get the full context. God has made us to be a kingdom and priests and therefore are deserving of crowns.

Exodus 29:1-9 describes the consecration of the priests of Israel. Verse 6 "and you shall set the turban on his head and put the holy crown on the turban." The priests are given holy crowns to wear.

Exodus 39 gives a description of priestly garments. Verse 30, "They made the plate of the holy crown of pure gold and inscribed it like the engravings of a signet, "Holy to the LORD." They fastened a blue cord to it to fasten it on the turban above, just as the LORD had commanded Moses."

The 24 elders have golden crowns because they have been made priests to God and golden crowns are a part of the priestly garments. Furthermore, "He has made us to be a kingdom and priests . . .". (Rev. 1:6). All those who accept Christ as their Lord and Savior are made priest and will have priestly crowns.

Around the throne are also 7 lamps of fire burning before the throne, which are the seven Spirits of God. John saw Jesus standing among seven lamp stands in Chapter 1 of Revelation. The seven lamp stands were identified as seven churches. The seven lamps is the Holy Spirit found in the church which works through the church to illuminate the world with the Light of Christ.

Around the throne are also four living creatures. They are described as:

Full of eyes front and back
One like a lion
One like a calf

One with the face of a man
One like a flying eagle
Six wings

This is the first time we have run into something strange and unfamiliar. It does not mean that it has some symbolic or exotic meaning just because it is strange and unfamiliar. Our intention is to use literal interpretation to the greatest extent possible. Using this approach we must believe that before the throne are four living creatures that are exactly as described. As we try to understand more about the creatures we find they are full of eyes, front and back. Their eyes do not miss anything. Nothing escapes their notice. They have six wings which can carry them, with great speed, anywhere they need or desire to go. They, in fact, know everything that is going on in all creation, being able to see all, and they are ever-present in all creation, having six wings to carry them in an instant to every corner of the world.

So, who or what are the four living creatures? First of all, they are four living creatures just as they are described and they are before the throne worshipping and praising God. But, beyond this, there is significance to their form.

Ezekiel writes about a vision where he sees four living beings resembling those John writes about in Revelation. "As for the form of their faces, each had the face of a man, all four had the face of a lion on the right and a bull on the left, and all four had the face of an eagle." (Ezek. 1:10). Each of the four animal forms seen in Ezekiel is the same as that seen in Revelation.

Isaiah saw the living creatures in his vision. "I saw the Lord sitting on a throne, lofty and exalted, with the train of His robe filling the temple. Seraphim stood above Him, each having six wings: with two he covered his face, and with two he covered his feet, and with two he flew." (Isa. 6:1-2). Ezekiel and Isaiah both see four living creature before the throne of God similar in appearance to the four living creatures in Revelation.

Is there significance to these four living creatures? In the beginning God created all things. In the beginning the earth was formless and void and darkness was over the surface of the deep. On the first day God created light. On the second day God made the heaven above the earth. On the third day God separated the waters and dry land appeared and God caused the earth to sprout vegetation. On the fourth day God created the sun and moon and stars. On the fifth day God created the fish and the birds. On the sixth day God created man and all the animals. On the seventh day God rested from all He had done. Genesis 2:20 further describes God's creatures. The man gave names to all the cattle, and to the birds of the sky, and to every beast of the field. Note that the five types of creatures of creation were the birds and fish and domestic animals and wild animals and man. Of these five, God brought only the warm blooded animals before Adam to name; the birds, the domestic animals, and the wild animals.

The four living creatures before the throne in Revelation 4 have the face of a lion, the face of a calf, the face of a man, and the face of an eagle. All of the warm blooded creatures of God's creation; wild animals, tame animals, birds, and man are seen before the throne worshipping and praising God. "day and night they (four living creatures) do not cease to say, "Holy, holy, holy is the LORD God, the Almighty who was, who is and who is to come."" (Rev. 4:8).

The twenty four elders fall prostrate before the throne worshipping God Almighty who lives forever and ever, they cast their crowns before the throne saying, "Worthy are You, our Lord and our God, to receive glory and honor and power; for You created all things, and because of Your will, they existed and were created." (Rev. 4:9-11). The twenty four elders cast their crowns before the throne because they are not worthy to receive glory, and honor and power. Only God, who is the eternal creator of all creation is worthy to receive such honor.

Chapter 4 sets the stage for John's second vision. He is in heaven and he is before the throne of God. He is in the very presence of God. He sees, around the throne, the four living creatures, all of God's creation, worshipping God and giving glory to Him. Further, he sees the twenty four elders before the throne also worshipping and giving glory to God.

John is in prison. He has seen great persecution of the church. He has experienced trials and tribulation for the sake of the gospel. The state of the church is not what it should be. God is sovereign over all things yet He allows His creation to turn from Him. "Therefore be careful how you walk, not as unwise men but as wise, making the most of your time, because the days are evil." (Eph. 5:15). "always giving thanks for all things in the name of the Lord Jesus Christ to God, even the Father." (Eph. 5:20). Paul says we are to give thanks to God in all things. We live in a fallen world with evil all around us. We are, in fact, subjected to the evil of this world and the effects of sin. Storms destroy our homes and cities, sickness weakens our spirit, death brings us great sorrow, weeds infest our gardens, men persecute us and murder and rob our brethren, we experience hatred, stress, anxiety, hopelessness, and despair. But, all in all, we know that God is with us and will not forsake us. "And we know that God causes all things to work together for good to those who love God, to those who are called according to His purpose." (Rom. 8:28). We can know that God is in control and He will provide for us no matter what this world offers. God and only God is worthy to be praised in spite of this fallen and debased world in which we live. No matter what situation we find ourselves in, no matter how bad things seem, in the end we will rise victorious. We will win.

The vision John is about to experience is not a pleasant one. Everything God has created will be destroyed in the end. All sin and evil and the effects of sin and evil must be destroyed in order for God to recreate a perfect world free of all sin and evil. There will be trials and tribulations for God's people. They will experience wars, famine, natural disasters, demonic plagues, and many will be killed for the sake of the gospel. But, we are able to look forward to the end and know that all these things must take place before we can receive our inheritance and live in God's new creation void of all sin and evil forever and ever.

All creation is praising and worshipping God because of what He has done, for what He is doing and for what He will do in the future.

Questions Chapter 4

John's second vision

Read through Revelation chapter 4 through 17:2. Read as though what you read is literal. As you do this assignment try to avoid using footnotes and chapter headings. Use only the text of Scripture.

This is John's second vision.

1. Where does this vision take place?

2. What is this vision about?

3. List major events of the vision

4. What are the three sets of sevens in the vision and what do you think they represent

5. Draw a time line showing the sequence of the events in John's second vision.

Read Revelation chapter 4

6. Who is sitting on the throne?

7. Who or what is around the throne?

8. How are the twenty four elders described?

9. Why were they clothed in white? See Revelation 3:18, 3:4, 3:5, Matthew 17:2, Mark 9:3,

10. Why did they have golden crowns? See Psalm 103:4, Exodus 29:1-9, Exodus 39:30, Revelation 1:4-6

11. Who do you think the 24 elders are? See Matthew 19:28, Luke 22:30, Psalm 122:4-6, Daniel 7:9, 13-14, Revelation 4:10, 5:6, 5:8, 5:14, 19:4 Twenty four elders are found nowhere else in Scripture.

12. In the center of the throne were four living creatures.

Describe each creature also see Ezekiel 1:1-12

13. Does Isaiah 6:1-2 give us a clue about the four living creatures?

14. Is there a relationship between the four living creatures in Revelation and Ezekiel and the living creatures, beings of Genesis chapter one?

15. What does God's Word say regarding the living creatures in Genesis 2:20?

16. What are the categories that are described?

17. Does this give us a clue to the four living creatures in Revelation?

18. Who or what are the seven spirits of God? Think this one through. The lamp stands are the churches. The seven spirits are the fire of the lamps burning before the throne.

19. What were the twenty four elders doing?

20. What were the four living creatures doing?

CHAPTER 5

Who is Worthy?

Read Chapter 5 of Revelation

"**I** saw in the right hand of Him who sat on the throne a book written inside and on the back, sealed up with seven seals. And I saw a strong angel proclaiming with a loud voice, "Who is worthy to open the book and to break its seals?" And no one in heaven or on the earth or under the earth was able to open the book or to look into it. Then I began to weep greatly because no one was found worthy to open the book or to look into it; and one of the elders said to me, "Stop weeping; behold, the Lion that is from the tribe of Judah, the Root of David, has overcome so as to open the book and its seven seals.""" (Rev. 5:1-5). John stands before the throne and the One on the throne has a book in His hand, written inside and on its back, and sealed with seven seals. A strong angel proclaims with a loud voice, "Who is worthy to open the book and break its seals?"

What do we suppose the book is; the Book of the Law or Covenant of Moses, Book of Chronicles, Book of Life, Book of the Words of Jeremiah, or the books talked about in Daniel?

"Now at that time Michael, the great prince who stands guard over the sons of your people, will arise. And there will be a time of distress such as never occurred since there was a nation until that time; and at that time your people, everyone who is found written in the book, will be rescued. Many of those who sleep in the dust of the ground will awake, these to everlasting life, but the others to disgrace and everlasting contempt. Those who have insight will shine brightly like the brightness of the expanse of

45

heaven, and those who lead the many to righteousness, like the stars forever and ever. But as for you Daniel, conceal the words and seal up the book until the end of time; many will go back and forth and knowledge will increase." (Dan. 12:1-4). The book written about in Daniel has been sealed up until the end of time. Daniel predicts a time of distress will occur prior to the end. And at the end, the book will be opened and those whose name is found in the book will be rescued. The book that is about to be opened is the book spoken of in Daniel 12.

The prophet Ezekiel is given a scroll and on it, front and back, was lamentation, mourning, and woe. See Ezekiel 2:8-10. Note that the book in Revelation is written inside and on its back. The seals of the book must be broken in order to get to the inside of the book. The seals bring lamentation, mourning, and woe. The time of distress that has never occurred before, spoken of in Daniel, is now about to be revealed to John.

Who is worthy to break the seals and open the book? How is He identified?

> "Lion that is from the tribe of Judah, the root of David." (Rev. 5:3-5).

> "Then a shoot will spring from the stem of Jesse and a branch from his roots will bear fruit." (Isa. 11:1).

> "Behold, days are coming, declares the Lord, when I will raise up for David a righteous Branch" (Jer. 23:5).

> "I am going to bring in My servant, the Branch." "Behold a man whose name is Branch" (Zech. 3:8, 6:12).

> "He will be great and will be called the Son of the Most High; and the Lord God will give Him the throne of His father David". (Lk. 1:32).

> "And so, because he was a prophet and knew that God had sworn to him with an oath to seat one of his descendants on his throne, he looked ahead and spoke of the resurrection of the Christ, that He was neither abandoned to hades, nor did His flesh suffer decay." (Acts 2:30-32).

"concerning His son, who was born of a descendant of David according to the flesh." (Rom. 1:3).

"Remember Jesus Christ, risen from the dead, descendant of David." (2 Tim. 2:8).

"I, Jesus, have sent My angel to testify to you these things for the root and descendant of David the bright and morning star." (Rev. 22:16).

Jesus is clearly the Lion from the tribe of Judah, the root of David. Jesus is the One identified as being worthy to open the book. Why is He worthy? What did He overcome?

Matthew 4:1-8 records that Jesus was carried into the wilderness and tempted by Satan with every temptation possible. We will never face any temptation that Jesus has not already faced. He fully and completely resisted all the temptation Satan could put before Him.

Hebrews 4:15 says we have a High Priest who, "has been tempted in all things as we are, yet without sin."

"Remember Jesus Christ, risen from the dead, descendant of David." (2 Tim. 2:8).

Jesus overcame all the temptations of the world, He went to the grave and was resurrected. He broke the bond of sin and death. His death paid the penalty for all the sins of the world. Because He lives those who accept Him as their Lord and Savior will also live. Jesus holds the keys to death and Hades. Jesus gives life to the dead. He alone is worthy to open the book.

"And I saw between the throne (with the four living creatures) and the elders a Lamb standing, as if slain, having seven horns and seven eyes, which are the seven Spirits of God, sent out into all the earth. And He came and took the book out of the right hand of Him who sat on the throne. When He had taken the book, the four living creatures and the twenty-four elders fell down before the Lamb, each one holding a harp and golden bowls full of incense, which are the prayers of the saints. And they sang a new song, saying, "Worthy are You to take the book and to break its seals; for You were slain, and purchased for God with Your blood men from every tribe and tongue and people and nation. "You have made them to be a kingdom and priests to our God; and they will reign upon the earth." (Rev. 5:6-10).

John sees a Lamb appear before the throne along with the four living creatures and the twenty-four elders. The Lamb was standing as if slain. The Lamb has seven horns and seven eyes which are the seven spirits sent out into the world. Jesus, when He was resurrected, gave His disciples the charge to go into all the world and make disciples of all nations, baptizing them in the name of the Father and the Son and the Holy Spirit. See Matthew 28:19-20. The development of the church unfolds as we read through the book of Acts. The Jews by and large reject the gospel of Christ and the Gentiles are brought into the fold. By the end of the book of Acts churches have been established in Asia Minor from Macedonia to Jerusalem. The gospel which started as a way of salvation for the Jews has now been opened to every tribe, and tongue, and people and nation. The charge of the church is now to spread the gospel message throughout the rest of the world. The seven churches in Revelation chapters 2 and 3 are representative of all the churches in the world. The Lamb with, seven horns and seven eyes, which are the seven spirits of God, empowers the church with the Holy Spirit to take the message to every tribe and tongue and people and nation.

The Lamb takes the book from the right hand of Him who sat on the throne. And the four living creatures and twenty-four elders fall down before the Lamb and each of them has a bowl full of incense which are the prayers of the saints. All the prayers of the saints are held in heaven for final disposition by the four living creatures and the twenty-four elders. It is not that the prayers have not been heard and it is not that the prayers have not been answered. God hears all of our prayers and He answers all prayers. But, even though they have been answered for our time, they still await a final disposition. All of our prayers, other than prayers of praise and thanksgiving, deal with overcoming the evil that is in the world. They deal with our pain and suffering, anxiety, grief, stress, relationships, physical needs, spiritual needs, protection and care of others, disaster relief, and bountiful crops, and personal and world peace. All of the things we pray for are prayers for relief from the effects that sin has brought upon the world. While the specific need we have is answered, the prayer is remembered for a time when all the prayers of the saints will be disposed of in their entirety. Finally, our prayers will be answered for all time when all evil is destroyed and it no longer affects our lives.

And the four living creatures and twenty-four elders fall down and worship the Lamb for He is worthy to break the seals on the book. Why is He worthy? He is worthy because He has purchased men from every tribe and tongue and people and nation and made them to be a kingdom and priests to our God, and they will reign upon the earth. He is worthy because He has redeemed those to be revealed by the book and these will rule with Him on this earth.

"Then I looked, and I heard the voice of many angels around the throne and the living creatures and the elders; and the number of them was myriads of myriads, and thousands of thousands, saying with a loud voice, "Worthy is the Lamb that was slain to receive power and riches and wisdom and might and honor and glory and blessing." And every created thing which is in heaven and on the earth and under the earth and on the sea, and all things in them, I heard saying, "To Him who sits on the throne, and to the Lamb, be blessing and honor and glory and dominion forever and ever." And the four living creatures kept saying, "Amen." And the elders fell down and worshiped." (Rev. 5:11-14).

John looks and he hears the voice of many angels around the throne. Not only are the four living creatures and twenty-four elders worshipping and praising the Lamb but there are myriads and myriads (thousands and thousands) of angels raising their voices in praise as well. Their praise is, "Worthy is the Lamb that was slain to receive power and riches and wisdom and might and honor and glory and blessing." The voice is described as a loud voice. The sound would have been deafening as they proclaimed their praise before the throne.

Not only does John see the twenty-four elders, four living creatures and thousands of angels praising the Lamb but he also sees every created thing which is in heaven and on the earth and under the earth and on the sea, and all things in them, lift up their voices in praise saying, "To Him who sits on the throne, and to the Lamb, be blessing and honor and glory and dominion forever and ever." John must be looking forward to a time beyond the seals and to a time when all evil has already been destroyed as John now sees all of creation worshipping and praising God and the Lamb. John now sees a glimpse of the final end when everyone, everything, and all creation have been recreated and understand the sovereignty and power and might and relentless love of our God and our Savior.

Questions Chapter 5

Read Revelation chapter 5

1. What is the book?

2. The Word "book" is used 173 times in Scripture. When it is used what is it referring to? You don't need to research all 173 places. Look at the passages below and identify the book in each of the references.

    Genesis 5:1

    Exodus 17:14

    Exodus 32:33

    1 Kings 14:19

    2 Kings 22:11

    2 Kings 23:2

    Nehemiah 13:1

    Psalm 69:28

    Psalm 139:16

    Daniel 7:10

    Revelation 3:5

    Revelation 5:1

3. In the references above what things are referred to by the name book?

4. What does Revelation 3:7 say about Jesus?

5. What does it mean, "the key of David"?

6. How does one enter the kingdom? See John 14:6

7. Who has the authority to allow one into the kingdom?

8. Who is worthy to open the book? See Revelation 5:5

9. What is the significance of opening the book? See Revelation 20:12-15; 21:26-27

10. What does the book reveal?

11. Do we know whose name is in the book before it is opened?

12. Whose name can you be certain is in the book?

13. Opening the book requires opening seven seals. What happens when the seventh seal is broken? See Revelation 8:1,2,6

14. What happens when the seventh trumpet is blown? See Revelation 11:15

15. What does it mean, "the kingdom of our world has become the kingdom of our Lord"? See Revelation 10:7

16. What is the mystery? See Mark 4:11, Romans 16:25, 1 Corinthians 15:51, Ephesians 3:1-12

Read Revelation 5:6

17. What are the seven horns and seven eyes?

Read Deuteronomy 33:17

18. What do the horns do?

Read the following

Psalm 92:10

Zachariah 1:21

Luke 1:69

19. What do you think the horns represent?

20. Read the following and record what the eye is:

Genesis 3:5

Numbers 24:15

Deuteronomy 21:9

Psalm 19:8

Proverbs 21:2

21. From what you have read what do you think the seven horns and seven eyes represent?

Read Revelation 5:8

22. What were the 24 elders and four living creatures holding?

Read 2 Chronicles 20:28, Psalm 33:2, Psalm 71:22,

23. Why did the 24 elders and four living creatures have harps?

Read Psalm 142:1, Exodus 30:8, Luke 1:10, Revelation 8:3,4

24. What did you learn about incense and prayer?

Read Revelation 5:1, Ezekiel 2:9,10

25. What was written outside the book? See Isaiah 29:11, Daniel 12:4

26. Why was the book sealed?

Read Revelation 5:11-14

27. Who was around the throne?

28. What were they doing?

29. Aside from the ones around the throne what else is praising Jesus?

30. Who is worthy to open the book and why?

31. Read chapters 6-8:5. Review your sequence chart developed last week. Make any refinements that you see regarding these chapters.

32. In as few Words as possible describe each event in chapters 6-8:5. Use only one Word if possible. For instance the red horse brings war. One Word to describe this event is war.

CHAPTER 6

The Tribulation

Chapters 6 through 11 in the book of Revelation describe the great tribulation. The tribulation period begins with the opening of the first seal when the Antichrist comes to bring peace to Israel and the tribulation period ends with the blowing of the last trumpet when the church is taken up to heaven. During this time many will be saved. This is God's last call. At the sound of the last trumpet there will be no more opportunity to be saved. God will remove the church from the earth and will execute His wrath upon the rest. All will die and the Antichrist and False Prophet will be thrown into the lake of fire. Satan will be bound for 1000 years. Then the church will be resurrected to inhabit the earth and reign with Christ for 1000 years. At the end of the 1000 years the dead will be raised and Satan will lead them to attack the saints. They will be destroyed with hail, fire, and brimstone and Satan will be thrown into the lake of fire. Then God will pronounce judgment on mankind. Those who are found guilty will be thrown into the lake of fire with the Antichrist, the False Prophet, and Satan. All evil will have been destroyed and the old heaven and earth will pass away. No remnants of evil will remain. A New Heaven and New Earth will appear, and we will live with God forever and ever.

The book of Revelation is God's plan for the establishment of His kingdom. It is given to us in sufficient detail that when the time comes we will recognize it and know that victory is on the horizon. This will be a difficult time. The tribulation that comes upon the world will affect both the righteous and the unrighteous. Those who are alive during this time will experience wars, famine, death, natural disasters and demonic plagues. But they will persevere through this time.

There are many prophecies concerning these end times. The 70th week of Daniel is often used to provide a time line for this period. Most scholars agree that the 70 weeks of Daniel represent seventy, seven year periods or 490 years.

Scripture often uses a week to refer to seven years. For instance, Jacob served Laban seven years and was given Leah to be his wife and then served another seven weeks, or seven years, and was given Rachel to be his wife. Genesis 29:27 reads, "Fulfill the week of this one and I will give thee the other also for the service which thou shalt serve me yet seven other years." Further, in Ezekiel 4 we read, "Moreover lie thou upon thy left side, and lay the iniquity of the house of Israel upon it; according to the number of the days that thou shalt lie upon it, thou shalt bear their iniquity. For I have appointed the years of their iniquity to be unto thee a number of days, even three hundred and ninety days: so shalt thou bear the iniquity of the house of Israel. And again, when thou hast accomplished these, thou shalt lie on thy right side, and shalt bear the iniquity of the house of Judah: forty days, each day for a year, have I appointed it unto thee." Again Scripture refers to days as years. However, the best way to confirm that Daniel's week refers to seven years is to realize that Daniel's prophecy has been fulfilled over a period of 70 weeks of years or 490 years as shown in the following.

Daniel

9:24   "Seventy weeks decreed for holy city to finish transgression"

> Israel will have 490 years to return to God. Seventy weeks equals 490 days. One day equal to one year, thus 490 years.

"To make an end to sin"

> To determine to live righteously

"To make atonement for iniquity"

> To repent of their sin

"To bring everlasting righteousness"

To establish everlasting righteousness

"To seal up the prophecy"

To complete the prophecy concerning the Messiah. Once the Messiah has come there will be no more prophecy concerning the Messiah.

"To anoint the holy place"

To anoint the Messiah with the Holy Spirit.

9:25   "from issuing of decree to restore and rebuild Jerusalem

Until Messiah the prince

There will be 7 weeks and 62 weeks"

From the decree issued by Artaxerxes until the Messiah is revealed and begins His ministry is 483 years. 7+62=69 ; 69 weeks X 7 days = 483 days. One day = one year thus 483 years. The first 7 weeks or 49 years was the time required to rebuild the Jerusalem.

"It will built again with plaza and moat, even in time of distress

One who is decreed is poured out on one who makes desolate"

9:26   "After 62 weeks the Messiah will be cut off and have nothing"

After the city is rebuilt there will be 62 weeks or 434 years until the Messiah is revealed. When Jesus was baptized and His ministry was established He gave up everything and sought to proclaim Himself the Messiah to all Israel. He had no place to live and had only the provisions that God provided Him. He was rejected by His people.

"The people of the prince who is to come

Will destroy the city and the sanctuary

Its end will come with a flood

Even to the end there will be war

Desolations are determined"

The people of the prince to come are the people of the Messiah or all Israel. They are responsible for the destruction of Jerusalem and the temple because of their hardened hearts and refusal to accept the Messiah.

"Jerusalem, Jerusalem, who kills the prophets and stones those sent to her! How often I wanted to gather your children together, the way a hen gathers her chicks under her wings, and you were unwilling. Behold, your house is being left desolate!" (Matt. 23:37).

9:27   "He will make a firm covenant with the many for 1 week"

The Messiah promised to bring salvation the Israel. During the last 3 ½ years of His life He carried the gospel message to the Jews. After His death the message continued to be proclaimed to the Jews for another 3 ½ years. Then when Stephen was stoned the Jews were dispersed and the message was no longer concentrated on the Jews but Paul was converted and the gospel was then carried to the rest of the world. Thus for seven years the gospel was carried to the Jews and the promise fulfilled.

"In the middle of the week He will put a stop to sacrifice and grain offering"

> After 3 ½ years of His ministry Jesus was crucified. His death was the ultimate sacrifice. The death of Jesus on the cross atoned for the sins of all people for all time. Every sin of the past was paid for, every sin of the present is paid for, and every sin of the future is already paid for with the precious blood of Jesus. God has provided His own sacrifice in His Son and no other sacrifice could be made. In fact further sacrifice after the crucifixion of Jesus would be an abomination to God.

"On the wing of abominations will come one who makes desolate

Even to a complete destruction"

> The Jews continued the sacrifice. after the death of Jesus on the cross To continue the sacrifice after the death of Jesus would say that the death of Jesus was of no value. This is an abomination to God. In 70 AD the temple and Jerusalem is completely destroyed. The temple would not to be rebuilt until the time of the end. God put a stop to the abomination in the temple.

This is an abbreviated view of the fulfillment of the seventieth week of Daniel. The seventieth week of Daniel therefore represents a period of seven years. Many scholars have applied the seventh week of Daniel to the end times. The following shows how the relationship of the 70th week of Daniel to Revelation may be understood.

"The people of the prince who is to come will destroy the city and the sanctuary

Its end will come with a flood even to the end there will be war

Desolations are determined" (Dan. 9:26)

> When applied to end times, the prince to come is the Antichrist. His people are those who follow him. Their refusal to accept Christ as the Messiah will bring a final destruction on Jerusalem and in fact the entire world.

"He will make a firm covenant with many for a week." (Dan. 9:27)

> The Antichrist will rule for 7 years. He will promise peace for Israel and will rebuild the temple

"In the middle of the week he will put a stop to sacrifice and grain offerings. On the wing of abominations will come one who makes desolate even to complete destruction." (Dan. 9:27)

> After 3 ½ years the Antichrist will declare himself God and stop the sacrifice in the temple. Following this abomination, the Antichrist declaring himself to be God, Satan will come and bring complete destruction.

According to Daniel chapter nine the end time tribulation period will be seven years. This is the time line that we will use as we apply what we learn from Revelation to a sequential time frame.

Using the Jewish calendar a year is 360 days, 7 years is 2520 days. The middle of the week occurs after 1260 days. We will see that the Antichrist appears on the scene at the opening of the first seal. He comes promising peace for Israel. He sees the temple rebuilt. Then after 3 ½ years, the middle of the week, he puts a stop to the sacrifice, declaring himself to be God. This begins the blowing of the first trumpet. After another 3 ½ years Jesus returns to call the church home. Following the removal of the church from earth, God brings His wrath on the world. This begins the pouring out of the seven bowls of wrath. This period will last 30 days.

/seven seals/seven trumpets/pouring out of seven bowls of wrath/

1260 days   1260 days   30 days

(See full time line in the appendix)

The period of tribulation, the seven seals and the trumpets will last 2520 days. The last 30 days is a period of wrath. The church will experience the great tribulation but will be removed before the wrath of God. "For they themselves report about us what kind of reception we had with you, and how you turned to God from idols to serve a true living God, and to wait for His son from heaven, whom He raised from the dead, that is Jesus, who rescues us from the wrath to come." (1 Thess. 1:9-10). "In a moment, in the twinkling of an eye, at the last trumpet, for the trumpet will sound, and the dead in Christ will be raised imperishable, and we will be changed." (1 Corinthians 15:52) "For the Lord Himself will descend from heaven with a shout, with the voice of the archangel and with the trumpet of God, and the dead in Christ will rise first. Then we who are alive and remain will be caught up together with them in the clouds to meet the Lord in the air, and so we shall always be with the Lord." (1 Thess. 4:16-17).

Read Matthew 24:1-31

Jesus gives us an outline of the end times.

Many false prophets will come
You will hear of wars and rumors of wars
There will be famines

There will be earthquakes

This is not the end but the beginning of birth pangs

Then you will be delivered to tribulation
You will be martyred and hated
Many will leave the faith
People will betray each other
People will hate each other
There will be many false prophets
Lawlessness will increase
Most people's love will grow cold

Those who persevere to the end will be saved

The gospel will be preached in the whole world
Then the end will come.

When the abomination of desolation spoken of in Daniel appears in the temple there will be a great tribulation such as has never occurred before.

The days will be cut short for the sake of the elect.
Many false prophets will arise
'Immediately after the tribulation of those days
    The sun will darken
    Moon will cease to shine
    Stars will fall from the sky
The sign of the Son of Man will appear in the sky
    The Son of Man will come on the clouds in the
    sky with power and great glory
He will send forth His angels and with a great trumpet
they will gather His elect

This passage describes the events that we will see unfold in Revelation from the opening of the seals to the blowing of the last trumpet.

The Scriptures are full of prophecies concerning the end times. Everything in Scripture is holy, inspired, infallible, and inerrant. That is, it is all true. Scripture supports Scripture. There are no inconsistencies. We cannot simply make Scripture say what we want it to say. "No prophecy of Scripture is a matter of one's own interpretation, for no prophecy was ever made by an act of human will, but men moved by the Holy Spirit spoke from God." (2 Peter 1:20). As we go forward we must be certain that we do not distort Scripture by adding to or taking away from its meaning. "I testify to everyone who hears the Words of prophecy of this book: if anyone adds to them, God will add to him the plagues which are written in this book; and if anyone takes away from the Words of the book of this prophecy, God will take away his part from the tree of life and from the holy city, which are written in this book." (Rev. 22:18-19). This is a dire warning and not to be taken lightly. Scripture says what Scripture says. The next 17 chapters in Revelation contain some difficult passages. We will continue to apply a literal interpretation to the rest of Revelation as we have the previous 5 chapters. When we read and accept Scripture for what it says the Holy Spirit will lead us and give us understanding.

Read Chapter 6 of Revelation

FIRST SEAL

"Then I saw when the Lamb broke one of the seven seals, and I heard one of the four living creatures saying as with a voice of thunder, "Come." (Rev. 6:1a). This, obviously, is Jesus. Throughout the book of Revelation John refers to the Lamb. In Chapter 5 He is standing as if slain and being worshipped. In Chapter 6 He is the One who opens the seals and is the object of fear for the unrighteous. In Chapter 7 He is being worshipped and is depicted as the Savior. In Chapter 8 He breaks the seventh seal. In Chapters 12 and 13 He is depicted as Savior. In Chapter 14 He is standing on Mt Zion, depicted as Savior, and witnesses judgment. In Chapter 15 He is being worshipped. In Chapter 17 He is the overcomer. In Chapter 19 He comes to join the church in marriage and becomes one flesh with them, and He hosts the marriage supper. In Chapter 21 He is the One who will marry the church and the One the apostles followed and He is the Temple and Light of the New Jerusalem. In Chapter 22 He sits on the throne. Jesus is at the center of everything that happens in the book of Revelation. He is the Savior. He is our Savior. He purchased the church with His blood. He judges the unrighteous. He is the One worthy of worship. He is the One who will join the church in marriage and become one flesh with them. He is the One who sits on the throne. He is worthy!

The Lamb breaks six of the seals in Chapter 6. In Matthew 24 we saw Jesus speak of these six seals saying there will be many false prophets, wars and rumors of war, famines and earthquakes. But, He says, the end is not yet, this is the beginning of birth pangs. In other Words things are going to get a lot worse. The opening of the first seal begins the countdown to the end. There will be seven more years and then the end of the world, as we know it, will come and then a new world will emerge void of the evil and corruption of the present world. We are told to pay close attention to the signs of the end times so we will be prepared and able to persevere through these times. The book of Revelation begins, "The Revelation of Jesus Christ, which God gave Him to show His bond servants, the things which must soon take place . . . . Blessed is he who reads and those who hear the Words of the prophecy, and heed the things which are written in it, for the time is near." (Rev. 1:1-3). As the angel gives the message to the seven churches he says over and over again, "He who has an ear, let him hear what the Spirit says to the churches." The context of this is not to simply hear the Words of the prophecy but rather to understand the prophecy. Those who have an ear are those who submit to the Holy Spirit for understanding and open themselves up to hear God speak. At the end of the book of Revelation Jesus says, "I, Jesus, have sent My angel to testify to you these things for the churches. I am the root and the descendent of David, the bright and morning star. The Spirit of the bride says "Come." And the one who hears says, "Come." And let the one who is thirsty come; let the one who wishes take the water of life without cost." (Rev. 22:16-17). This prophecy is given to us so that we will recognize the coming of the tribulation and will be able to prepare ourselves as best we can in order that we might persevere through to the end.

Our first indication that the end is near is the breaking of the first seal. "The Lamb broke one of the seven seals . . . . and behold, a white horse, and he who sat on it had a bow; and a crown was given him, and he went out conquering and to conquer." (Rev. 6:2). Who is this rider on the white horse? The one on the white horse comes to conquer the world. He comes riding a white horse promising peace but he carries a bow in order to wage war. He is given a crown. He is a powerful world leader. He is the

Antichrist. He promises to bring peace to Israel but the "peace" will last but a short 3 ½ years. He will decree that the temple be rebuilt in Jerusalem and he will make it possible for the Jews to again bring their sacrifice to the temple. After 3 ½ years, in the middle of the week, he will put a stop to the regular sacrifice. He will declare himself to be god and demand that he be worshipped. This is the abomination of desolation as found in the prophecy of Daniel 8:9-14 and Daniel 9:25-28. Jesus says, "When you see the abomination of desolation which was spoken of through Daniel the prophet, standing in the holy place let the reader understand, then those who are in Judea must flee to the mountains." (Matt. 24:15-16). Our first positive sign that the end is near is the coming of the Antichrist who is identified as the one who promises peace for Israel and initiates the rebuilding of the temple. When the rebuilding of the temple begins we know the end is near. "From the rebuilding of the temple to the end will be 2300 evenings and mornings." (Dan. 8:9-14). In the middle of the week we will see the abomination of desolation standing in the temple. When this happens, be ready for 3 ½ years of turmoil and destruction.

SECOND SEAL

"When He broke the second seal, I heard the second living creature saying, "Come." And another, a red horse, went out; and to him who sat on it, it was granted to take peace from the earth, and that men would slay one another; and a great sword was given to him." (Rev. 6:3, 4). The peace promised by the Antichrist will last but a very short time. Then all the world will break out in war. No one will find a safe haven, there will be no peace. "They heal the brokenness of the daughter of My people superficially, saying, "Peace, peace." But there is no peace." (Jer. 8:11). The prophet Jeremiah says that peace will be promised to Jerusalem but the peace is only on the surface and soon goes away only to be replaced with turmoil and war. Jesus also spoke of this, "You will hear of wars and rumors of wars . . . . For nation will rise up against nation, and kingdom against kingdom." (Matt. 24:6-7). There are always wars someplace on the earth but this will be different. This will be a time of widespread wars. No nation will be at peace, except that Israel will remain at peace for the first 3 ½ years. Note that Jesus says "You will hear of wars and rumors of wars." Israel will hear of the wars all around but will not participate in the wars.

THIRD SEAL

"When He broke the third seal, I heard the third living creature saying, "Come." I looked and behold, a black horse; and he who sat on it had a pair of scales in his hand. And I heard something like a voice in the center of the four living creatures saying, "A quart of wheat for a denarius, and three quarts of barley for a denarius; and do not damage the oil or the wine." (Rev. 6:5,6). The third rider brings famine and super inflation across the world. Jesus tells us that the wars will be followed by famines, "For nation will rise up against nation, and kingdom against kingdom, and in various places there will be famines and earthquakes." (Matt. 24:7). At this point the famines are not world-wide but are in various places. They are certainly much greater than the famines in various parts of the world today. They are so significant that the whole world will be shaken by the short supply of food and even those who have food will pay dearly to get enough to eat.

FOURTH SEAL

"When the Lamb broke the fourth seal, I heard the voice of the fourth living creature saying, "Come." I looked, and behold, an ashen horse; and he who sat on it had the name Death; and Hades was following with him. Authority was given to them over a fourth of the earth, to kill with the sword and with famine and with pestilence and by the wild Beast of the Earth." (Rev. 6:7,8). The fourth rider brings death to ¼ of the earth. The population today is approximately 6 billion 930 million. ¼ of this is 1 billion 731 million people. So when the fourth seal is broken almost 2 billion people will be killed. Some will be killed with the sword, some will die of starvation, some will die of sickness and some will be eaten by wild animals that most likely are also starving for lack of food.

FIFTH SEAL

"When the Lamb broke the fifth seal, I saw underneath the altar the souls of those who had been slain because of the Word of God, and because of the testimony which they had maintained; and they cried out with a loud voice, saying, "How long, O Lord, holy and true, will You refrain from judging and avenging our blood on those who dwell on the earth?" And there was given to each of them a white robe; and they were told that they should rest for a little while longer, until the number of their fellow servants and their brethren who were to be killed, even as they had been, would be completed also." (Rev. 6:9-11). At the opening of the fifth seal John sees the souls of all those who have maintained their faith and continued to proclaim the gospel message even to the point of death. The martyrs are reminded of God's promise, "Rejoice, O nations, with His people; for He will avenge the blood of His servants, and will render vengeance on His adversaries, and will atone for His land and His people." (Deut. 32:43). God has promised that He will bring vengeance upon those who destroy His faithful children. The martyrs are now crying out, "How long will you refrain from judging them?" They are told to wait and rest a while but when the numbers of those yet to be killed for their faith is completed, then the vengeance will begin. The blowing of the last trumpet will call all the saints to heaven and then the vengeance will begin.

John refers to those who have killed the martyrs as those who dwell on earth. There are only two kinds of people; those who dwell on earth and those who dwell in heaven. Those who dwell on earth put all their faith and trust in earthly things. For them the importance of life lies in their happiness and they do whatever they can in order to have a life full of fun, material things, and money. They go after any and everything that strokes their ego and satisfies their sensual desires. Those who dwell in heaven put their faith and trust in heavenly things. They live today for the promise of eternal life with God. They are only passing through this earthly realm on their way to their final destination in heaven. Their purpose in life is to glorify God. Their life is not about satisfying their own earthly pleasures. It is about bringing glory and honor and praise to God. The focus of their lives is on heavenly things.

John refers to those who dwell on earth many times in Revelation. This is done to the exclusion of those who dwell in heaven. "Those who dwell on earth will face the hour of testing." (Rev. 3:10). Those who dwell in heaven will not. "Those who dwell on earth killed the martyrs." (Rev. 6:10). Those who dwell in heaven did not. "Those who dwell on earth will experience the final three woes." (Rev. 8:13). Those who dwell in heaven will be protected during this time. Those who dwell on earth rejoiced over the killing of the witnesses as the witnesses tormented them." (Rev. 11:10). Not so for those who dwell in heaven. "Those who dwell on earth worship the Beast and are deceived by the Beast and make an idol of the Beast."

(Rev. 13:8, 14). Not true for those who dwell in heaven. Those who dwell on earth will wonder when they see the Beast." (Rev. 17:8). Those who dwell in heaven will understand. As we read through the rest of Revelation let the reader understand that when John refers to those who dwell on earth he is not making reference to all the people who remain and are alive on earth. He is referring only to those who have not accepted the gospel of Christ and so remain focused on the things of this earth.

The martyrs are given white robes. Jesus refers to those in white robes as those who overcome the temptations of this world and remain faithful to the end. To the church at Sardis He says, "the people in Sardis have not soiled their garments; and they will walk with Me in white, for they are worthy. He who overcomes will thus be clothed in white garments; and I will not erase his name from the book of life, and I will confess his name before My Father and before His angels." (Rev. 3:4-6). No man is righteous in his own right. "All have sinned and fall short of the glory of God." (Rom. 3:23). Therefore none are righteous. But Christ has redeemed the elect. He has covered their sin with His own blood. They have been washed and made clean. Paul writes to the church at Corinth, "Do you not know that the unrighteous will not inherit the kingdom of God? Do not be deceived; neither fornicators, nor idolaters, nor adulterers, nor effeminate, nor homosexuals, nor thieves, nor the covetous, nor drunkards, nor revilers, nor swindlers, will inherit the kingdom of God. Such were some of you; but you were washed, but you were sanctified, but you were justified in the name of the Lord Jesus Christ and in the Spirit of God." (1 Cor. 6:9-11). There is no sin that will prevent us from inheriting the kingdom of God if we accept Christ as our Lord and Savior. Even though we may have committed some of the sins listed that would keep us from inheriting the kingdom of God if we accept Christ as our Lord and Savior He will wash us and sanctify us and justify us before God and will not remove our name from the book of life.

How long will it be until the martyrs are avenged? The martyrs are told to wait a little longer until their numbers are complete. "then the angel whom I saw standing on the sea and on the land lifted up his right hand to heaven, 'and swore to Him who lives forever and ever, who created heaven and the things in it, and the earth and the things in it and the sea and the things in it, that there will be delay no longer, but in the days of the voice of the seventh angel (blowing of the seventh trumpet), when he is about to sound, then the mystery of God is finished, as He preached to His servants the prophets." (Rev. 10:5-7). What follows the blowing of the seventh trumpet begins the avenging of the blood of the martyrs. The question, "How long will it be?", will be answered with the blowing of the seventh trumpet. The delay will then be over.

SIXTH SEAL

"I looked when He broke the sixth seal, and there was a great earthquake; and the sun became black as sackcloth made of hair, and the whole moon became like blood; and the stars of the sky fell to the earth, as a fig tree casts its unripe figs when shaken by a great wind. The sky was split apart like a scroll when it is rolled up, and every mountain and island were moved out of their places. Then the kings of the earth and the great men and the commanders and the rich and the strong and every slave and free man hid themselves in the caves and among the rocks of the mountains; and they said to the mountains and to the rocks, 'Fall on us and hide us from the presence of Him who sits on the throne, and from the wrath of the Lamb; for the great day of their wrath has come, and who is able to stand?'" (Rev. 6:12-17). The breaking of the sixth seal brings terror on all the earth. But the end is not yet. Jesus says, "You will hear of wars and rumors of wars, see that you are not frightened . . . . that is not the end . . . . there will be famines and earthquakes. But these things are merely the beginning of birth pangs. Then they will deliver you to tribulation" (excerpts from Matt. 24:4-9). As bad as this time seems, it is not yet the end. Following this time there will be a period of great tribulation. Will the saints be here for the tribulation period? Jesus said, "Then they will deliver you to tribulation." So yes, the saints will be delivered to a time of tribulation. But before that, at the opening of the sixth seal, there will be a great earthquake, the sun will turn black, the moon will turn red as blood, the sky will be split apart, every mountain and island will be moved out of its place and things, as bad as things are, they are about to get worse.

THE RAPTURE

There is much discussion about the rapture. Will there be a rapture? If so, will it be before the tribulation, in the middle of the tribulation, or at the end of the tribulation?

"And inasmuch as it is appointed for men to die once and after this comes judgment, so Christ also, having been offered once to bear the sins of many, will appear a second time for salvation without reference to sin, to those who eagerly await Him." (Heb. 9:27), Jesus will come again to gather those waiting for Him.

"The Sun darkened, the moon will not give its light, stars fall, powers of heaven shaken then: He comes on the clouds and sends His angels to gather His elect from the farthest end of the earth to the farthest end of heaven." (Mark 13:24-26).

"Everyone will not die but everyone will be changed. In the twinkling of an eye, at the last trumpet the dead will be raised imperishable and those alive will be changed. The perishable body will be made imperishable and the mortal body immortal." (1 Cor. 15:51-52).

"Jesus will come and raise up all His elect on the last day." (John 6:39). That is, once Jesus comes to gather His elect, He will gather them all at one time. There will be no further opportunity for salvation.

Jesus will, "descend from heaven with a shout, with the voice of an archangel and with the trumpet of God and the dead in Christ will rise first then those who are alive and remain will be caught up together with them in the clouds to meet the Lord in the air." (1 Thess. 4:16).

There will be a rapture. There will be a future time when Christ will come to gather His elect. They will all be gathered at the same time, both the dead and the living. The dead in Christ have already been spiritually raised and their spirit is now in heaven with Jesus. But at the last trumpet they will be bodily raised. He will come at the sound of the last trumpet and there will be no further opportunity for salvation for those who remain. The timing for His coming is at the sound of the last trumpet. His elect will remain on earth for the opening of the seals and for the sound of the first six trumpets. At the sound of the seventh trumpet Christ will return to gather His elect from every corner of the earth and above the earth and below the earth. This is a bodily resurrection. The souls of those who died previously are already in heaven. Christ will gather the souls of the dead along with their bodies and the living souls and bodies and they will be changed into new bodies fit for the kingdom of God.

A perfect outline of the events leading up to the rapture is given in Mark 13:6-37. The sequence given by Jesus is:

False prophets will come

There will be many wars

There will be famines

There will be martyrs

The gospel will be preached everywhere

The abomination of desolation will be revealed

There will be a great tribulation

The days will be shortened

After the tribulation the sun darkens, the moon darkens, stars fall, powers are shaken

The Son of Man comes and gathers His elect

Scripture is clear. There will be a period of tribulation. After the tribulation Jesus will return to gather His elect. After the tribulation God will pour out His wrath on all that remain. God's elect will be protected from the wrath of God but they will face the tribulation.

Questions Chapter 6

Read chapter 6

1. How is the One who broke the seals described? See Revelation 6:1, 7, 9

2. Look up the following references to the Lamb in Revelation and record what the Lamb is doing

   Revelation 5:6

   Revelation 5:8

   Revelation 5:12-13

   Revelation 6:16

   Revelation 7:10

   Revelation 7:14

   Revelation 7:17

   Revelation 8:1

   Revelation 12:11

   Revelation 13:8

   Revelation 14:1

   Revelation 14:4

   Revelation 14:10

   Revelation 15:3

   Revelation 17:14

   Revelation 19:7

   Revelation 19:9

   Revelation 21:9

   Revelation 21:14

Revelation 21:22-23

Revelation 22:1,3

3. Why do you think John uses the term Lamb for Jesus?

4. What is the mission of the white horse and its rider?

5. What is his weapon?

6. What is the purpose of the bow and arrow?

7. What events follow the rider on the white horse?

8. Who do you think the rider is?

9. What did the second seal bring?

10. What was the mission of the rider on the Red Horse?

11. What did the third seal bring?

12. What did the rider of the Black Horse bring?

13. What did the forth seal bring?

14. What did the rider of the Ashen Horse bring?

15. What was revealed with the breaking of the fifth seal?

16. Why were the martyrs killed?

17. What was the question posed by the martyrs?

18. What was the answer?

19. What must happen before the judgment can take place?

20. Who are those who dwell on the earth?

    Revelation 3:10

    Revelation 6:10

    Revelation 8:13

    Revelation 11:10a

    Revelation 11:10b

    Revelation 13:8

    Revelation 13:14a

    Revelation 13:14b

    Revelation 17:8

21. What is the significance of the white robes?

    Revelation 3:4-5, 18

    Revelation 4:4

    Revelation 6:11

    Revelation 7:9

    Revelation 19:14

22. When will the avenging take place? See Revelation 10:5-7

23. What happened when the sixth seal was broken?

24. Using as few Words as possible, perhaps one, describe the events of the first seal. And do the same for each seal in the first column. Read Matthew 24:5-14 and record the events in the second column that seem to match the first column.

Revelation 6   Matthew 24

2. _____   5. _____

4. _____   6. _____

56. _____   7. _____

8. _____   9a. _____

9. _____   9b. _____

12._____   _____

CHAPTER 7

Interlude

Read Chapter 7 of Revelation

"*A*fter this I saw four angels standing at the four corners of the earth, holding back the four winds of the earth, so that no wind would blow on the earth or on the sea or on any tree. And I saw another angel ascending from the rising of the sun, having the seal of the living God; and he cried out with a loud voice to the four angels to whom it was granted to harm the earth and the sea, saying, "Do not harm the earth or the sea or the trees until we have sealed the bond-servants of our God on their foreheads." (Rev.7:1-3). The opening of the seventh seal begins the great tribulation. There will be great suffering during this time. Those who dwell on earth (the unsaved) will suffer unbearable torment and pain. Those who dwell in heaven (the saved) will also experience the effects of the tribulation but they will be protected from the full and direct impact of the events to follow the opening of the seventh seal.

John looks around and he sees four angels at the four corners of the earth holding back the four winds of the earth so that no wind would blow on the earth or on the sea or on any tree. Another angel cries out with a loud voice saying, "Do not harm the earth or sea or the trees until I have sealed the bond servants of our God on their foreheads." The events that follow the opening of the seventh seal will be either natural disasters or supernatural torment and destruction. The four angels have put a hold on the tribulation until God's chosen have been sealed for protection during this time.

"And I heard the number of those who were sealed, one hundred and forty-four thousand sealed from every tribe of the sons of Israel: from the tribe of Judah, twelve thousand were sealed, from the tribe of Reuben twelve thousand, from the tribe of Gad twelve thousand, from the tribe of Asher twelve thousand, from the tribe of Naphtali twelve thousand, from the tribe of Manasseh twelve thousand, from the tribe of Simeon twelve thousand, from the tribe of Levi twelve thousand, from the tribe of Issachar twelve thousand, from the tribe of Zebulun twelve thousand, from the tribe of Joseph twelve thousand, from the tribe of Benjamin, twelve thousand were sealed." (Rev. 7:4-8). Who are the ones who are sealed for protection? There are 144,000; 12,000 from each tribe of the sons of Israel. If we go back to Genesis 35 we read that the twelve sons of Jacob are Reuben, Simeon, Levi, Judah, Issachar, Zebulon, Joseph, Benjamin, Dan, Naphtali, Gad, and Asher. Curiously, one of the original tribes of Israel, Dan, is missing and another tribe, Manasseh (Joseph's first son), is put in his place. Reading in Numbers 34:13-29 we find a list of tribes that were apportioned land in the Canaan. This list is the same as the 12 sons of Jacob except that the tribe of Levy was not given land, as they were the priestly tribe, and in their place Joseph's sons, Ephraim and Manasseh, were each given ½ portions.

God has chosen to protect his people during the time of the tribulation. The tribe of Levy is included in this protection but God has omitted Dan and Ephraim. We can easily understand that God would protect His priestly tribe during this time, but why exclude Dan and Ephraim? Looking at Genesis 49:17 Dan is referred to as a "serpent in the way, a horned snake in the path, that bites the horse's heels, so that the rider falls backward." Scripture uses snake or serpent as a reference to evil or Satan. The tribe of Dan has turned to evil ways, even influencing the rest to turn from the One true God. And then, in Judges 18:30-31, we read that the tribe of Dan set up idols for worship at Shiloh and became idol worshippers. Therefore, as the tribe of Dan has turned away from God, God has excluded them from protection in these end times and they have lost their inheritance in the kingdom of God.

The tribe of Ephraim, which was given a half portion of land in Canaan, was also excluded from God's protection. In reading Hosea 4:17-19, we find that Ephraim also has turned to idol worship. And so again, the tribe of Ephraim is excluded because they too have turned to idol worship and forsaken the one true God.

So, of the original twelve sons of Jacob all are represented except for Dan. Dan was excluded because his tribe turned away from God to idol worship. And Manasseh, Joseph's first son, has taken his place. Revelation 7 tells us that the angels sealed 12,000 from each of the tribes. Before the seventh seal is opened the angels must protect this special group of Israel by placing the seal of God on their foreheads. Are there really 12,000 from each tribe or is the number 12,000 a representative number of perfection or completeness? Our approach to this study is to interpret everything as literal as possible. As we are given no indication that the number is anything other than 12,000, to put some other meaning to this would be to read into Scripture something that is not there. We could as easily question if there were really 12 sons of Jacob or if the time of creation was really 6 days with one day of rest. So for the purpose of this study we will assume that John heard that the number to be sealed was 144,000, 12,000 from every tribe of the sons of Israel. God will mark with His seal 12,000 from each tribe of Israel before the tribulation can begin

This 144,000 are not necessarily all of the Jewish people that will be saved during the tribulation period. This is a very special group. If we go forward to Revelation 14:1-7 we learn more about who these particular Jews are. They have the name of Jesus and the name of His Father on their foreheads. That is, they were sealed. They were singing a new song before the throne of God which no one could learn except the 144,000. "These are the ones who have not been defiled with women, for they have kept themselves chaste. These are the ones who follow the Lamb wherever He goes. These have been purchased from among men as first fruits to God and to the Lamb. And no lie was found on their mouth; they are blameless." We will discuss these 144,000 in greater detail when we get to Chapter 14. But for now let it suffice that they are a very special group of Jews who have been singled out to be protected because of their unyielding faith and dedication to God.

Are these the only ones protected during this time? What about the rest of Christians? "Now He who establishes us with you in Christ, and anointed us in God, who also sealed us and gave us the Spirit in our hearts as a pledge." (2 Cor. 1:21-22). "In Him, you also, after listening to the message of truth, the gospel of your salvation – having also believed, you were sealed in Him with the Holy Spirit of promise." (Eph. 1:13). And, "Do not grieve the Holy Spirit of God, by whom you were sealed for the day of redemption." (Eph. 4:30). Those who accept Christ are sealed by the Holy Spirit for the day of redemption. They will be protected during the tribulation by virtue of their seal.

After these things John looked and saw "a great multitude, which no one could count, from every nation and all tribes and peoples and tongues standing before the throne and before the Lamb, clothed in white robes, and palm branches were in their hands; and they cry out with a loud voice, saying, "Salvation to our God who sits on the throne, and to the Lamb." And all the angels were standing around the throne and around the elders and the four living creatures; and they fell on their faces before the throne and worshiped God" (Rev. 7:9-11). John sees a great multitude, all the angels, the 24 elders and the four living creatures standing before the throne. They all fell on their faces before the throne of God and worshipped Him saying, "Amen, and blessing and glory and wisdom and thanksgiving and honor and power and might, be to our God forever and ever, Amen." (Rev. 7:12).

There is a great multitude that no one could count. This gives us great comfort to know that there will not be just a select few who will be saved but there will be a great multitude, a group so large that no one was able to count them all. This group is not from just a select group of people. There are people from every nation, tribe, peoples and tongues. No one is excluded because of their race, sex, religion, nationality or origin. Everyone has the opportunity to accept Christ and be counted in the numbers of the saved. Those before the throne are clothed in white robes. Only the righteous are given white robes. Do we deserve to wear a white robe? No. There is none righteous, not even one. How then is there a great multitude before the throne clothed in the white robe of righteousness? Paul, in writing to the church at Corinth says this, "but you were washed, but you were sanctified, but you were justified in the name of the Lord Jesus Christ and in the Spirit of our God." (1 Cor 6:11). Those who accept Christ as their Lord and Savior are washed, and sanctified, and justified in the name of Jesus. No matter what they may have done in the past, no matter how vile or wicked they may have been, they are now new creatures in Christ Jesus and worthy of the white robe of righteousness.

They are before the throne waving palm branches and giving praise to God. Why do they wave palm branches? In Leviticus 23 we get a description of the Feast of Tabernacles or Booths. At the onset of the feast the people are directed by God to gather palm branches and to wave them before the LORD. The feast is thus ushered in by the waving of the palm branches. As we will see in just a minute John is getting a glimpse of the time when the final Feast of Booths is about to begin.

One of the elders asked John, "Those who are clothed in the white robes, who are they and where have they come from?" John answered, "My lord, you know." And the elder replies, "These are the ones who come out of the great tribulation, and they have washed their robes and made them white in the blood of the Lamb." (Rev. 7:13-14). Who are the ones clothed in white? These are the ones who come out of the great tribulation. The great tribulation commences with the blowing of the first trumpet and ends with the blowing of the last trumpet. At the sound of the last trumpet Jesus will return to earth on a cloud and the dead in Christ will rise to meet Him in the air, then those who are alive will be caught up together with them to meet the Lord in the air. (1 Thess. 4:16-17). When the first trumpet blows there will be people here on earth who are saved and there will be people who are not saved. During the great tribulation period many will be martyred. They will refuse the mark of the Beast and will not be able to buy or sell. Some will die because they refuse to deny Jesus. Some will die because they cannot buy food or water. They will see many of their friends and neighbors killed. But some will persevere through this time and will not lose their faith. This is the last opportunity for everyone. This is God's last call to redemption. Many will be angry and afraid and will curse God for bringing such devastation upon the earth. But, also, many will recognize the power and grace and mercy of God and will turn to Him for their salvation. At the blowing of the last trumpet it will be done. All those who are saved or will be saved have been removed from the earth. They will be spared the wrath of God which is about to come to all who remain.

"For this reason they are before the throne of God; and they serve Him day and night in His temple; and He who sits on the throne will spread His tabernacle over them. They will hunger no longer, nor thirst anymore; nor will the sun beat down on them, nor any heat; for the Lamb in the center of the throne will be their shepherd, and will guide them to springs of the water of life; and God will wipe every tear from their eyes." (Rev.7:15-17). Those who come out of the great tribulation are before the throne of God praising Him and rejoicing. They have been removed from the hunger and thirst and burning sun of the great tribulation and are now protected in the tabernacle of God. They need worry no more. Jesus will be their shepherd. He will provide for their every need. He will lead them to springs of the water of life, and God will wipe every tear from their eyes. There will be no more pain, no more suffering, no more sadness, no more worry, no more anxiety, no more stress, no more of anything that upsets them or brings them worry or discomfort. They are in God's tabernacle and under His care and protection.

QUESTIONS CHAPTER 7

Read Revelation Chapter 7:1-8 and 14:1-5

1. What were the four angels doing?

2. Why were the twelve tribes sealed?

3. What do you learn about the 144000?

Read Genesis 35:23-29

4. Who are the 12 sons of Jacob?

5. How do these compare to Revelation?

Dan has been replaced with Manasseh.

Read Genesis 41:51

6. Who is Manasseh?

Read Genesis 49:17 and Judges 18:30-31

7. What does this tell us about Dan?

8. Why do you think Dan is excluded in the tribes mentioned in Revelation 7?

Read Hosea 4:17-19

9. What does this say about Ephraim?

10. Why do you think Ephraim is not included in Revelation 7?

Read Numbers 34:13-29

11. Which tribes were apportioned land?

Read Joshua 14:4

12. Who got the portion of land that would have gone to the tribe of Levy?

Using the list developed in Numbers and omitting Dan and Ephraim because of their idol worship and restoring Levy and Joseph you have the 12 tribes listed in Revelation 7

Read Revelation 12:9-10

13. What made up the great multitude?

14. Were these Jews only?

15. Where were they?

16. How were they clothed?

17. What were they doing?

18. Is there any relation to Leviticus 23:34-40?

19. Where did the great multitude come from?

20. What did they do to be able to stand before the throne? Revelation 5:9

21. What benefit do they gain? Revelation 7:16-17; Isaiah 25:8;

Revelation 21:3-4;

22. What happens in Revelation chapter 8?

23. What happens in Revelation chapter 9?

24. What happens in chapter 10?

25. What happens in chapter 11? See Revelation 11:15

26. What happens in chapter 12?

27. What happens in chapter 13?

28. What happens in chapter 14?

29. What is happening in Revelation 14:15-16

30. What is happening in Revelation 14:17-18?

31. Draw a timeline of the seven trumpets; Revelation 8-14

CHAPTER 8

Four Trumpets

Read Revelation Chapter 8

"**W**hen the Lamb broke the seventh seal, there was silence in heaven for about half an hour. And I saw the seven angels who stand before God, and seven trumpets were given to them." (Rev. 8:1-2). When the Lamb breaks the seventh seal there is silence in heaven for one half hour and seven angels standing before the throne are given seven trumpets. The great tribulation is about to begin. "Be silent before the Lord God! For the day of the LORD is near . . . . Near is the great day of the LORD! . . . . A day of wrath is that day, a day of trouble and distress, a day of destruction and desolation, a day of darkness and gloom, a day of clouds and thick darkness, a day of trumpet and battle cry . . . . I will bring distress upon men so they will walk like the blind because they have sinned against the LORD and their blood will be poured out like dust . . . . neither their gold or silver will be able to deliver them on the day of the LORD's wrath; and all the earth will be devoured in the fire of His jealousy, for He will make a complete end, indeed a terrifying one, of all the inhabitants of the earth." (Zeph. 1:7-18). The prophecy of Zephaniah concerning the end times says it begins with a time of silence. Be silent! Wait and watch for the end is near. And then in Deuteronomy 27:9 "Then Moses and the Levitical priests spoke to all Israel, saying, "Be silent and listen, O Israel! This day you have become a people for the Lord your God."" Be silent! Pay attention! Something very important is about to happen. Before the great tribulation begins, before the earth is purged of all evil, before the people of God will be able to live in peace, there is a period of silence. God is about to redeem His people and restore His creation. Be silent and wait.

"Another angel came and stood at the altar, holding a golden censer; and much incense was given to him, so that he might add it to the prayers of all the saints on the golden altar which was before the throne. And the smoke of the incense, with the prayers of the saints, went up before God out of the angel's hand. Then the angel took the censer and filled it with the fire of the altar, and threw it to the earth; and there followed peals of thunder and sounds and flashes of lightening and an earthquake." (Rev. 8:3-5). What just happened is very significant. The angel has a censer full of the prayers of all the saints. The prayers went up before God out of the angel's hand. The prayers of all the saints are about to be answered. This will not be a temporal event. The prayers of the saints will not be answered this day just so they will be faced with another day of troubles. This is a final answering of all the prayers of all the saints for all time.

There are generally three types of prayer: prayers of thanksgiving; prayers of praise; and prayers of petition. Prayers of thanksgiving and praise do not need a response from God. They are our way of recognizing His grace and mercy in our lives. However, prayers of petition and intercession anticipate that God will respond in some way to provide for our needs or the needs of someone else. It seems that we are in continual need of God's provisions for ourselves, our family or someone else. These needs are brought upon us as a result of sin, not necessarily our sin but rather they also may be the result of sin in general. For instance, sickness, famine, natural disasters, weeds, draught, aches, pain, death and the like are all brought about by God's judgment on the world for sin. It is not that we experience these things because of our sin. Rather, our lives are affected by God's general judgment on the world. We did nothing personally to bring about a storm, sickness, or famine but these things are a part of God's judgment on the world. We are often affected by the destruction and hardships they bring. But, sometimes it is our own sin that brings judgment. Our greed can bring unmanageable debt that brings stress and anxiety and illness. Our unfaithfulness in marriage can bring guilt, and stress, and financial ruin. Our reckless disregard for life can bring about sickness, disability, or death. In other words, sin in our own lives can and often does bring about pain and hardship. All of the troubles of life are brought about by either the effects of our own sin, the sin of someone else, or they are the effects of God's judgment on the world for the original sin in the Garden of Eden. And our prayers of petition are lifted up as we seek relief from the pain and difficulties of life brought about by sin. All of life's tribulations are brought about by sin and evil in the world.

John sees an angel with a censer full of the prayers of the saints. All of the prayers of all times are being lifted up to be answered. Today our prayers are answered one by one as we lift them up to God. However, sin still exists in the world and abounds in our lives so troubles and difficulties continue to plague us. What is about to happen is the prayers of all the saints are about to be answered once and for all time. Sin and evil and its effects are about to be removed from all the earth forever. Without sin and evil there will be no more of life's difficulties and we will be free of pain, sorrow, anxiety, stress, disappointment, and all of the things that make our lives miserable. After the removal of sin and evil on the earth, a New Heaven and a New Earth appear and God will live among His people, "and He will wipe away every tear from their eyes; and there will no longer be any death; there will no longer be any mourning, or crying, or pain; the first things have passed away." (Rev. 21:1-4). The final answer to all our prayers is not that God helps us through the difficulties of life as He does today only to have more difficulties tomorrow. The final answer is that all the difficulties of life are removed from us forever.

This earth has been corrupted by sin since the very first sin in the Garden of Eden. Man had the opportunity to choose to do good or to do evil. Man chose to disobey God. As a result, all of mankind has been under the curse of sin. Man learned to lie, cheat and steal. Hatred filled his heart. Greed blinded his eyes. Lust consumed his mind. His every thought and deed became evil. There are none who do good, not even one. Sin has affected not just mankind but his whole world. Weeds make it difficult for the flowers to grow. Fires destroy our forests. Floods erode the land. Wild animals live in fear of man. All of nature suffers at the hand of corruption. But God has redeemed for Himself a people. All of those who accept Christ as their Lord and Savior have been redeemed. Sin no longer has power over their lives. Today they live in an alien world. Though they have been redeemed and their hearts have been changed, their minds still desire the things of this world. Sin abounds even in the lives of the redeemed. Yet, God gives hope to His people. God promises a life free from the miseries of this world. For those who remain faithful and persevere through this world, God has promised a new world free from sin and corruption. In order for God to accomplish His purpose He must first destroy the present world and all of its sin and corruption.

The seven trumpets are God's final call to redemption. During this time there will be a great tribulation far worse than any that has ever occurred before. Most will turn away from God and curse Him during this time but many will turn their hearts towards God and be saved. At the sound of the seventh trumpet God will remove His people from the earth. Then the wrath of God will be poured out on all that remain and the earth and everything in it will be destroyed. All evil will be destroyed, Satan, the False Prophet, and the Antichrist will be thrown into the lake of fire, and a New Heaven and a New Earth will appear free from corruption and God will live with His people and He will provide their every need. All the prayers of all the saints will have been answered for all time.

"And the seven angels who had the seven trumpets prepared themselves to sound them." (Rev. 8:6). Thus begins the great tribulation.

The first four trumpets destroy one third of creation. "The first sounded, and there came hail and fire, mixed with blood, and they were thrown to the earth; and a third of the earth was burned up, and all the green grass was burned up." (Rev. 8:7). The first trumpet destroys one third of the vegetation. "The second angel sounded and something like a great mountain burning with fire was thrown into the sea; and a third of the sea became blood, and a third of the creatures which were in the sea and had life, died; and a third of the ships were destroyed." (Rev. 8:8-9). The second trumpet destroys one third of the sea and everything in it. "A third angel sounded, and a great star fell from heaven, burning like a torch, and it fell on a third of the rivers and on the springs of water. The name of the star is called Wormwood; and a third of the waters became wormwood, and many men died from the waters, because they were made bitter." (Rev. 8:10-11). The third trumpet destroys one third of the fresh water supply. There will be no source of fresh water to drink. "The fourth angel sounded, and one third of the sun and one third of the moon and one third of the stars were struck, so that a third of them would be darkened and the day would not shine for a third of it, and the night the same way." (Rev. 8:12). The first three trumpets destroy one third of the earth; the land, the sea, and the rivers. The fourth trumpet destroys one third of the heavens.

There is a great significance to this fourth trumpet. What will follow the fourth trumpet are three woes. "Then I looked and I heard an eagle flying in midheaven, saying with a loud voice, "Woe, woe, woe to those who dwell on earth, because of the remaining blasts of the trumpet of the three angels who are about to sound!"'" (Rev. 8:13). Again, those who dwell on earth are the unsaved; those who put their faith and trust in worldly, earthly things. There are also on earth those who dwell in heaven, the saved. These put their faith and trust in heavenly things. Those who dwell in heaven will be protected by the mark of God on their foreheads but, even so, they will feel the effects of the three woes. Jesus says, "For those days will be a time of tribulation such as has not occurred since the beginning of the creation until now, and never will. Unless the Lord had shortened those days, no life would have been saved; but for the sake of the elect, whom He chose, He shortened the days." (Mark 13:19-20). Things have been bad so far during the great tribulation but things are about to become most unbearable as we will see. But God wants His elect to survive this time. So at the sound of the forth trumpet He shortens the days by one third. The sun will no longer shine for one third of the time and the night too has been shortened by one third. The twenty four hour day has become a sixteen hour day. The rest of the tribulation, though it will be much more intense, will only last two thirds as long.

Questions Chapter 8

Read Revelation chapter 8

1. What are the events of Revelation chapter 8?

2. What does the following say about being silent?

   Zephaniah 1:7

   Deuteronomy 27:9

   Lamentations 3:25-27

   Zechariah 2:13

   Psalms 65:1-3s

3. What would the seven trumpets given to the angels bring?

Read Revelation 8:3-5

4. What are the saints praying for? See Revelation 6:9-11

When we pray we ask God to intercede and do something for us:

5. What kind of things do you pray for?

6. What is the cause of the problem you pray for?

7. How might the problem be permanently resolved?

8. After the prayers are offered up what happens next?

9. What is initiated by the casting of the censer of fire to the earth?

Read Revelation 21:1-7

10. What is the result of purging the earth of evil and sin?

11. Why trumpets?

Read Genesis 1

12. What was created day 1?

13. What was created day 2?

14. What was created day 3?

15. What was created day 4?

16. What was created day 5?

17. What was created day 6?

18. What happened day 7?

Day three through six are related to the creation of the earth and everything on the earth. Review the trumpet judgments of trumpets one through six and see if they can be matched to what God created.

Draw a line from the trumpet to the day of creation where the thing being judged is created

Trumpet one

Trumpet two   Day 3

Trumpet three   Day 4

Trumpet four   Day 5

Trumpet five   Day 6

Trumpet six

19. Describe what happens when trumpet one is blown.

Read Revelation 16:9-11. This is related to the fourth bowl of wrath.

20. Who do men blame for the disaster?

21. Describe what happens when the second trumpet is blown.

22. What did John say was thrown into the sea? Was it a mountain?

23. Describe what happens when the third trumpet is blown

24. What do you think falls from heaven into the rivers?

25. What happened to the water?

26. Describe the events of the fourth trumpet

27. What happened to the day and the night?

Read Mark 13:19,20

28. Do you see a correlation between the fourth trumpet and what Mark said would happen?

29. What is going to follow the four trumpets?

30. So far God's judgment has affected only 1/3 of His creation. Why do you suppose He did not just destroy it all at once?

Trumpets Five and Six;
Locusts and the Army

Read Chapter 9 of Revelation

"Then the fifth angel sounded, and I saw a star from heaven which had fallen to earth; and the key to the bottomless pit was given to him. He opened the bottomless pit, and smoke went up out of the pit, like the smoke of a great furnace; and the sun and the air were darkened by the smoke of the pit. Then out of the smoke came locusts upon the earth, and power was given to them, as the scorpions of the earth have power. They were told not to hurt the grass of the earth, nor anything green, nor any tree, but only the men who do not have the seal of God on their foreheads. And they were not allowed to kill anyone, but to torment for five months; and their torment was like the torment of a scorpion when it stings a man. And in those days men will seek death and will not find it; they will long to die, and death flees from them." (Rev. 9:1-6). Remember that there are two groups of people on earth; those who dwell on earth, the unsaved, and those who dwell in heaven, the saved. The locust will only torment those who do not have the seal of God on their foreheads. Therefore it follows that at this time there are on earth those with the seal of God on their foreheads and those without the seal of God on their foreheads. God desires to protect His people from the effects of His woeful judgments therefore He has shortened the days.

God's first woe brings a great swarm of demonic, locust like creatures upon the earth to torture those who refuse to turn to God. There are so many locusts that the sun is darkened by their presence and the air is completely filled with them. Even the elect, those who dwell in heaven, will be affected by their presence. With such a large number of locusts everywhere and with them stinging and tormenting those without the mark of God, this time will be very stressful and disturbing for the elect. Even though they are not directly affected by the stinging, they will witness the suffering and torment of others, some of which may be their friends and family. They will see them even attempt suicide but to no avail.

The locusts were dreadful beasts. Their appearance was "like horses prepared for battle. On their head appeared to be crowns like gold, and their faces were like the faces of men. They had hair like the hair of women, and their teeth were like the teeth of lions. They had breastplates like breastplates of iron; and the sound of their wings was like the sound of chariots of many horses rushing for battle. They had tails like scorpions, and stings; and in their tail is the power to hurt men for five months. They have, as king over them, the angel of the Abyss; his name in Hebrew is Abaddon, and in the Greek He has the name Apollyon." (Rev. 9:7-11). Exactly who or what are the locusts? Their leader is the angel of the Abyss. Abaddon in Hebrew and Apollyon in Greek means destroyer. Their leader is either Satan or one of his angels. And the locusts themselves are demonic beings up out of the Abyss. Nothing has the power to stop the locusts. They march like a great army over the surface of the earth and no one without the seal of God on their forehead is safe from their pursuit. The only escape from the locusts will be to turn to God. Many will notice the protection that those with the seal of God on their foreheads have and will repent and turn to Him for salvation. But most will not.

After five months the locusts return to the Abyss. There is a brief period of peace and quiet. Those who dwell on earth were cursed by the locusts for five months yet they almost immediately forgot the torture they endured during that time and they immediately returned to their old ways, refusing to repent. "The first woe is past; behold two woes are still coming after these things." (Rev. 9:12).

The locusts come from and return to the Abyss. They are led by the angel of the Abyss. We live in a time in which there is a physical world, the earth, and two spiritual worlds, heaven and the Abyss. God resides in heaven along with His angels and heavenly beings and Satan resides in the Abyss along with his angels and demonic beings. Satan's influence on earth is strong today but it will get even stronger as we near the end.

"Then the sixth angel sounded, and I heard a voice from the four horns of the golden altar which is before God, one saying to the sixth angel who had the trumpet, "Release the four angels who are bound at the river Euphrates." And the four angels who had prepared for the hour and day and month and year, were released so that they would kill a third of mankind." (Rev. 9:13-15). At the opening of the fourth seal, 25% of mankind was killed. That leaves 75% of mankind. Now one third of these are to be killed. Thus, in all, one half of mankind is killed. With the population of the world today at around 7 billion people that means that with these two plagues there will be 3.5 billion people killed.

"The number of the armies of the horsemen was two hundred million; I heard the number of them. And this is how I saw in the vision the horses and those who sat on them: the riders had breast plates the color of fire and the hyacinth and of brimstone; and the heads of the horses are like the heads of lions; and out of their mouths proceed fire and smoke and brimstone. A third of mankind was killed by these plagues, by the fire and the smoke and the brimstone which proceeded out of their mouths. For the power of the horses is in their mouths and in their tails; for their tails are like serpents and have heads, and with them they do harm." (Rev. 9:16-19). We have never seen anything like this. We cannot imagine horses with heads like lions and fire and smoke and brimstone coming out of their mouths. But, maintaining our literal interpretation of Scripture we must accept this to be exactly what it says it is. Verse 15 tells us that four angels who were bound at the river Euphrates were released with the express purpose of killing one third of mankind. There is no indication that the horsemen are human. The mission is an angelic mission. God sends His angels across the face of the earth to kill one third of mankind just as He sent His angels through Egypt killing the first born of every man and beast. God's people, the saved, will be protected during this time. They will be in the midst of the destruction taking place but they will not be killed. They have the seal of God (covered by the blood of Jesus) which protects them just as the blood of the lamb on the door post protected the Israelites when the angel of death went through Egypt killing the first born of every man and animal before the Exodus. They will see their friends and neighbors and perhaps even some of their family cut down before their very eyes.

This is God's final call to repentance. With the first trumpet God sent hail and fire mixed with blood and one third of the earth was burned up. With the second trumpet God hurls a great burning mountain into the sea and one third of the sea becomes blood and one third of sea creatures die and one third of ships are destroyed. With the third trumpet a great star falls from heaven and one third of the rivers become bitter and unfit to drink. With the fourth trumpet the days are shortened in preparation for the three woes which are about to occur. With the fifth trumpet God sends locusts upon all the earth for five months to torture all those who dwell on earth, the unsaved. Now the sixth trumpet sounds and God sends a great army of angels to pass over the earth and kill one third of mankind. And even so, in the midst of all of this; "The rest of mankind who were not killed by these plagues, did not repent of the works of their hands, so as not to worship demons, and the idols of gold and of silver and of brass, and of stone and of wood, which can neither see nor hear nor walk; and they did not repent of their murders nor of their sorceries nor of their immorality nor of their thefts." (Rev. 9:20-21).

Since the creation, God's people, beginning with Adam, succumbed to the call of Satan and turned away from God. Even before the trumpets, since the creation, God has been calling His people to repentance. "Why then has this people, Jerusalem, turned away in continual apostasy? They hold fast to deceit, they refuse to return . . . . No man repented of his wickedness, saying "What have I done?" Everyone turned to his course . . . . The wise men are put to shame, they are dismayed and caught; behold they have rejected the Word of the LORD . . . . Everyone is greedy for gain . . . . Everyone practices deceit . . . . Were they ashamed because of the abomination they had done? They certainly were not ashamed, and they did not know how to blush . . . . Why have they provoked Me with their graven images, with foreign idols?" (Jer. 8:5-7). "And you will know that I am the LORD, when I bring you into the land of Israel, into the land which I swore to give to your forefathers. There you will remember your ways and all your deeds with which you have defiled yourselves; and you will loathe yourselves in your own sight for all the evil things that you have done. Then you will know that I am the LORD when I have dealt with you for My name's sake, not according to your evil ways or according to your corrupt deeds, O house of Israel," declares the Lord GOD."

(Ezek. 20:42-44). The entire Bible from Genesis to Revelation is focused on one purpose; God's call to repentance for His people. God desires for His people to repent and return to Him. Now the time for repentance is over. The next trumpet is the final woe. There will be no time left for the unrepentant.

QUESTIONS CHAPTER 9

Read Revelation chapter 9

Beginning of three woes, The Fifth Trumpet, Locusts

1. Who gave the key to the "star"? SeeRevelation 1:18

2. When the bottomless pit was opened what came out of it?

3. What do you learn about locusts in the following?

   Exodus 10:13-15

   Judges 8:15

   Jeremiah 46:23

4. What do you learn about scorpions in the following?

   Deuteronomy 8:14-16

   1 Kings 12:14

5. What were the locusts told to leave alone?

6. How long would the locusts torment men?

7. How will the people react?

8. Describe the locusts.

9. Who rules the locusts?

10. What or who is Abaddon? See Job 28:20-28; 31:1-12; 26:5,6; Proverbs 15:9-11; Proverbs 27:19-22

Abaddon

destruction, the Hebrew name (equivalent to the Greek Apollyon, i.e., destroyer) of "the angel of the bottomless pit" (Revelation. 9:11). It is rendered "destruction" in Job 28:22; 31:12; 26:6; Proverbs 15:11; 27:20. In the last three of these passages the Revised Version retains the Word "Abaddon." We may regard this Word as a personification of the idea of destruction, or as sheol, the realm of the dead.

Trumpet six

11. Where were the four angels that were released?

12. Where is the river Euphrates?

13. How many mounted troops were there?

14. How many people were killed? Today's world population is around 6.7 billion

15. Who kills the people?

16. What were the riders and horses like?

17. Read Revelation 6:7 How many were killed?

Of 100% this leaves 75%

18. How did they kill 1/3 of mankind?

    1/3 of 75% is 25% which leaves 50% So by now ½ of mankind has been killed.

19. What happened in Revelation 8:7?

20. What about those with the seal of God during this time?

21. What about the rest of mankind?

Read Jude verse 6; 2 Peter 2:4

22. Are these angels taking part in what is happening in Revelation 9?

CHAPTER 10

The Little Book

Read Chapter 10 of Revelation

Six trumpets have sounded. The seventh trumpet is about to blow. The seventh trumpet will initiate the rapture. All the saints will be removed. The only thing left will be to bring God's wrath on those who dwell on earth and complete the destruction of all evil. The time for repentance will be over once the seventh trumpet blows. Just a few things are left to do before the last angel blows the seventh trumpet. The first thing deals with the angel and the little book. "I saw another strong angel coming down out of heaven, clothed with a cloud; and the rainbow was upon his head, and his face was like the sun, and his feet like pillars of fire; and he had in his hand a little book which was open. He placed his right foot on the sea and his left on the land; and he cried out with a loud voice, as when a lion roars; and when he had cried out, the seven peals of thunder uttered their voices. When the seven peals of thunder had spoken, I was about to write; and I heard a voice from heaven saying, "Seal up the things which the seven peals of thunder have spoken and do not write them." Then the angel whom I saw standing on the sea and on the land lifted up his right hand to heaven, and swore by Him who lives forever and ever, WHO CREATED HEAVEN AND THE THINGS IN IT, AND THE EARTH AND THE THINGS IN IT, AND THE SEA AND THE THINGS IN IT, that there will be delay no longer, but in the days of the voice of the seventh angel, when he is about to sound, then the mystery of God is finished, as He preached to His servants the prophets." (Rev. 10:1-7).

The term "strong angel" is used three times in the book of Revelation. In chapter 5:1-3 the strong angel proclaims with a loud voice, "Who is worthy to open the book and break its seals?" The strong angel is one who commands authority. And in chapter 18:21 The strong angel hurls a millstone into the sea saying, "So will Babylon the great city, be thrown down in violence and will not be found any longer." And again the strong angel is one who commands authority. And here in chapter 10 the strong angel speaks with great authority concerning what is about to happen. The angel places his right foot on the sea and his left foot on land showing that he has authority over everything on earth and everything in the earth both land and sea.

After the angel spoke, the seven peals of thunder uttered their voices. In Exodus 19:19 we read, "When the sound of the trumpet grew louder and louder, Moses spoke and God answered him with thunder." And in Job 37:5, "God thunders with His voice wondrously, doing great things which we cannot comprehend." And in Psalm 29:3, "The voice of the LORD is upon the waters; the God of glory thunders, the LORD is over many waters." And God answers Job in Job 40:9, "Or do you have an arm like God, and can you thunder with a voice like His?" In this last reference God asks Job if he can thunder with a voice like His. No one is able to thunder with a voice like God. When John hears the seven peals of thunder he is hearing the very voice of God. We do not know what God said. John was told not to write it down but to seal it up.

And the angel lifts up his hand towards heaven and swore by God that the delay is over. When the last trumpet blows the mystery of God is finished. What is it that will not be delayed? When the fifth seal was broken in Revelation 6:9-11 John saw the martyrs under the altar crying out, "How long, O Lord holy and true, will you refrain from judging and avenging our blood on those who dwell on earth?" The avenging is about to begin. What we have seen so far has been bad. But what will follow the blowing of the last trumpet will be the wrath of God upon the earth and upon those who dwell on earth. Those who dwell in heaven will not be here. At the sound of the seventh, last, trumpet the mystery of God will be completed. Paul explains this mystery in 1 Corinthians 15:50-53, "Now I say this, brethren, that flesh and blood cannot inherit the kingdom of God; nor does the perishable inherit the imperishable. Behold, I tell you a mystery; we will not all sleep, but we will all be changed, in a moment, in the twinkling of an eye, at the last trumpet; for the trumpet will sound, and the dead will be raised imperishable, and we will be changed . . . . Death is swallowed up in victory. Death, where is your victory? O death, where is your sting? The sting of death is sin, and the power of sin is the law; but thanks be to God, who gives us the victory through our Lord Jesus Christ." Yes! The mystery of God is completed when the last trumpet blows and the dead in Christ are raised and changed to immortal beings and the ones alive are changed to immortal beings and we meet Jesus in the air and are removed from all evil forever and ever. We will not experience the wrath of God that is about to come upon those who dwell on earth. We will be taken up to heaven in preparation for God's final battle at Armageddon against those who dwell on earth.

"Then the voice which I heard from heaven, I heard again speaking with me, and saying, "Go take the book which is open in the hand of the angel who stands on the sea and on the land." (Rev. 10:8). When John asked for the book, the angel gave it to him and told him to take it and eat it. He said it would taste sweet in his mouth but would make his stomach bitter. When he took the book and ate it, it was sweet as honey in his mouth and when he had finished eating it his stomach was made bitter. This event is similar to the story of Ezekiel found in Ezekiel chapters 2 and 3. God sent Ezekiel to the sons of Israel to prophesy to them concerning their future. God handed him a scroll and on the scroll front and back were written lamentations, mourning, and woes. Ezekiel was told to eat the scroll and he ate it and it was sweet as honey in his mouth. There are many parallels in these stories. Both John and Ezekiel were given "scrolls" to eat. "So I went to the angel, telling him to give me the little book. And he said to me, "Take it and eat it; it will make your stomach bitter, but in your mouth it will be sweet as honey. I took the little book out of the angel's hand and ate it, and in my mouth it was sweet as honey; and when I had eaten it, my stomach was made bitter." (Rev. 10:9, 10). I took the little book out of the angel's hand and ate it, and in my mouth it was sweet as honey; and when I had eaten it, my stomach was made bitter. To eat something means more than just to read it. It means to make it a part of you. It means to take it in and digest it. Both John and Ezekiel found the scroll to be sweet as honey in their mouth. "And they *said to me, "You must prophesy again concerning many peoples and nations and tongues and kings." (Rev. 10:11). Ezekiel was told to deliver the message to the sons of Israel that if they did not turn from their wicked ways they would surely die and those who repent will surely live. For Ezekiel this was a message of hope. John is told to go and prophesy again concerning many peoples and nations and tongues and kings. John also saw a message of hope and found the scroll to be sweet in his mouth. But when he had digested it he found it to be bitter in his stomach. Knowing that those who repent will be saved is a sweet message but realizing that there will be many who do not repent and will be lost is a bitter message. John knew that many would not respond to the final call and would perish.

QUESTIONS CHAPTER 10

Six trumpets have sounded. We are getting ready to blow the seventh trumpet. The seventh trumpet will initiate the rapture. All the saints will be removed. The only thing left will be to bring God's wrath on those who dwell on the earth and complete the destruction of all evil. There is little time left for repentance. If anyone is going to accept Christ and be saved now is the time. This is the state of affairs for chapter 10.

Read Revelation chapter 10 with the above in mind.

The term strong angel is only used three times in Scripture all of them in the book of Revelation.

Read Revelation 5:1-3.

Read Revelation 10:1-3

Read Revelation 18:20-22

King James, NIV, Living Bible, says it is a mighty angel strong angel or mighty angel does not mean physically strong but it means one with great authority or one in a leadership position. It is an angel that is powerful and is assigned important duties.

Read Revelation 10:4

1. What or who is the seven peals of thunder?

2. Read the following and record who or what is the thunder.

   Exodus 19:19

   Job 37:1-5

   Job 40:9

Psalm 29:3

Read Ezekiel 2-3

3. What did the angel give to Ezekiel?

4. What did the angel give John?

5. What did the angel tell Ezekiel to do with it?

6. What did the angel tell John to do with the little book?

7. In the context of Ezekiel what did the angel mean "to eat the scroll?"

8. What was in the scroll?

9. What was in the scroll given to John? See Revelation 10:11

10. How did Ezekiel receive the scroll?

11. How did John receive the scroll?

12. What was Ezekiel to do with what he learned from the scroll?

13. What was John to do with what he learned from the scroll?

14. How would the people in Ezekiel respond?

15. How do we think the people responded to John?

Read Daniel 12:4-9

16. Is this the same book John is given to eat in Revelation 10?

Revelation Chapter 10:2 shows the angel has command over the earth and the seas.

Read Revelation10:6.

17. What was the message?

Read Revelation 6:9-11

18. What is not to be delayed?

Read Revelation 10:7

19. What is finished?

20. What is the mystery of God? See Mark 4:11; Romans 16:24-26

21. What is the mystery of God in the following?

Romans 11:24-26

1 Corinthians 15:50-52

Ephesians 3:1-10

Colossians 1:25-27

Revelation 10:9-10

22. Why does he eat the book or what does it mean to eat the book? See Ezekiel 2

23. What do you think makes the book sweet in John's mouth? Again refer to Ezekiel

24. What do you think makes it bitter in his stomach?

Read Revelation 10:11

25. What is John to do after he ate the book?

26. To whom is he told to prophecy?

27. After the sixth trumpet John is told to prophecy again. Is there someone still around to prophecy to and who would they be?

This prophecy is much like the prophecy Jonah was told to give to Nineveh. Jonah 3:1-4. But this is the last chance. Repent and be saved. Once the seventh trumpet blows it will be too late.

CHAPTER 11

Two Witnesses and the Seventh Trumpet

Read Chapter 11 of Revelation

"Then there was given me a measuring rod like a staff; and someone said, "Get up and measure the temple of God and the altar, and those who worship in it. Leave out the court which is outside the temple and do not measure it, for it has been given to the nations; and they will tread under foot the holy city for forty-two months." (Rev. 11:1-2). John is given a measuring rod and told to measure the temple of God, the altar, and those who worship in it. He is told to leave out the outer court because it has been given to the nations and they will tread underfoot the holy city for 42 months. Where is this temple? John is told not to measure the outer court which was given to the nations who will defile Jerusalem for 42 months. The temple therefore is in Jerusalem. We are not given a reason that John was to measure the temple but doing so shows that it has a real physical presence. John is also told to measure those who worship in the temple. As John is told to measure those who worship in the temple it stands to reason that the number of people who worship in the temple is a finite number, capable of being determined. These people are worthy to be counted. The fact that John is told not to measure the outer court shows that the outer court and those in the outer court are not worthy to be counted and are of no significance.

Several things will happen during this 42 month period. The holy city, Jerusalem, will be trampled by the nations (Rev. 11:2), two witnesses will rise up to prophesy for twelve hundred and sixty days concerning the final days (Rev. 11:3), the woman, Israel, will flee to the wilderness where she will be nourished for twelve hundred and sixty days (Rev. 12:6), and the Beast of the Sea will rise up and make war with the saints (Rev. 13:6-7 and Dan. 7:23-25).

For now we are concerned with the two witnesses. "And I will grant authority to my two witnesses, and they will prophesy for twelve hundred and sixty days, clothed in sack cloth. These are the two olive trees and the two lamp stands that stand before the Lord of the earth. And if anyone wants to harm them fire flows out of their mouth and devours their enemies; so if anyone wants to harm them, he must be killed in this way. These have the power to shut up the sky, so that rain will not fall during the days of their prophesying; and they have power over the waters to turn them into blood, and to strike the earth with every plague, as often as they desire." (Rev. 11:3-6). The two witnesses will prophesy concerning the end times and their message is the same message Jonah carried to Nineveh: if you do not repent of your evil ways God will destroy you. This is God's last call for repentance.

The two witnesses are clothed in sack cloth. Sack cloth was worn to show that they were in mourning. "So Jacob tore his clothes, and put sack cloth on his loins and mourned for his son many days." (Gen. 37:34). Ahab acted abominably by following idols. When Elijah pointed out to him his evil ways and told him how his actions would bring him great distress, "When Ahab heard these Words he tore his clothes and put on sackcloth." (1Kings 21:27). Ahab humbled himself before the LORD. The two witnesses were in mourning over Israel and God's people as they refused to repent and turn to God.

The witnesses will bring plagues upon the earth to show that God is displeased with what is happening. Perhaps the worst plague is the lack of rain for twelve hundred and sixty days. Without rain everything will turn to dust. Any fresh water that remains is turned to blood. There will be precious little to eat or drink. Yet, in spite of their pleas and in spite of the plagues the people will not repent.

The two witnesses are referred to as two olive trees and two lamp stands. "But as for me I am like a green olive tree in the house of God; I trust in the loving kindness of God forever and ever." (Ps. 52:8). The green olive tree in Psalm 52 is shown to be one who is patient in the midst of adversity trusting in the loving kindness of God. Zechariah the prophet has a vision of two olive trees which are one on the right and one on the left of a lamp stand. Zechariah asked the angel what the two olive trees were and the angel answered, "These are the two anointed ones who are standing by the Lord of the whole earth." (Zech. 4:14). The two witnesses are referred to as olive trees because they fully trust in God and will not be moved. They are anointed by God to do His work. They stand by God no matter what is going on around them. They are referred to as lamp stands because they carry the light of the gospel message to the world.

There is much speculation over who these two witnesses are. The Scriptures simply do not tell us. It may perhaps be best, in keeping with our intent to literal interpretation, to simply accept that we do not know, we only know that God rises up two people to be witnesses during these last days. However, I provide the following for consideration as to who these witnesses may be. Jesus says, "These are My Words which I spoke to you while I was still with you, that all things which are written about Me in the Law of Moses and the Prophets and Psalms must be fulfilled." (Luke 24:44) Saying in effect that the Law and the prophets are a witness as to who He is. And then, "Phillip found Nathanael and said to him, "We have found Him of whom Moses in the Law and also the Prophets wrote – Jesus of Nazareth." (John 1:45) This again shows that the Law and the Prophets testify to who Jesus is. And at the Mount of Transfiguration, Moses (the Law) and Elijah (the prophet) appear with Jesus. (Matt. 17:1-3). The Law testifies to who Jesus is as He fulfills every requirement of the Law. And the prophets testify to who Jesus is as they accurately foretell His coming. Scripture holds these two, the Law and the prophets, up as witnesses to who Jesus is. Our text says, "And I will grant authority to my two witnesses . . ." (Rev. 11:3). We could, therefore, surmise that the two witnesses are Moses and Elijah. However, they may also simply be two unknown witnesses whom God raises up in the last days as final witnesses to Jesus.

The two witnesses will be protected for forty two months during the time of their prophesying. No one will be able to harm them during this time. But, "When they have finished their testimony (When the forty two months have passed), the Beast that comes up out of the Abyss will make war with them, and overcome them, and kill them. And their dead bodies will lie in the street of the great city which mystically is called Sodom and

Egypt, where also their Lord was crucified. Those from the peoples and tribes and nations will look at their dead bodies for three and a half days and will not permit their dead bodies to be laid in a tomb. And those who dwell on the earth will rejoice over them and celebrate; and they will send gifts to one another, because these two prophets tormented those who dwell on earth". (Rev. 11:7-10).

Who is this Beast that comes up out of the Abyss? In Chapter 9 of Revelation we discovered that the ruler of the locusts was that angel of the Abyss or Satan. As the Abyss is the place where Satan and his angels and demonic beings reside, we can say that the Beast who comes and kills the two witnesses is Satan, probably the Antichrist. When they have been killed, "their dead bodies lie in the street of the great city mystically called Sodom and Egypt." By this time the great city, Jerusalem, has become a worldly place like Egypt and an immoral place like Sodom. John chooses Egypt and Sodom because Egypt is the most worldly and godless place he knew and Sodom was the most immoral place that had ever been. There is no mistaking that even Jerusalem, the holy city of God, has become evil and corrupt. The bodies lie in the streets three and a half days. Those from the peoples, tribes and nations (the saved who remain in Jerusalem) will not allow them to be buried. Note that Scripture often refers to those from the peoples, tribes, and nations as being all of God's people. The tribes are the twelve tribes of Israel but the peoples and nations refer to all the gentiles or non-Jews who have been saved. And those who dwell on earth (the unsaved) will rejoice over them.

"After three and a half days, the breath of life from God came into them, and they stood on their feet; and great fear fell upon those who were watching them. And they heard a loud voice from heaven saying to them, "Come up here." And then they went up to heaven in the cloud, and their enemies watched them. And in that hour there was a great earthquake, and a tenth of the city fell; seven thousand people were killed in the earthquake, and the rest were terrified and gave glory to the God of heaven." (Rev. 11:11-13). After three and a half days the bodies would surely have begun to stink. There would be no doubt that they were dead. There would be no doubt that God had resurrected them and called them to heaven. Their last great act as witnesses was to be resurrected and ascend to heaven after being dead for three and a half days. Seven thousand people were killed in the earthquake but those who survived and were watching this happen could not deny the power of God and some of them turned to God and were saved.

"The second woe is past; behold the third woe is coming quickly." (Rev. 11:14).

"Then the seventh angel sounded; and there were loud voices in heaven saying, "The kingdom of the world has become the kingdom of our Lord and of His Christ; and He will reign forever and ever." And the twenty four elders, who sit on their thrones before God, fell on their faces and worshipped God, saying, "We give You thanks O Lord God, the Almighty, who are and who were, because You have taken Your great power and have begun to reign." (Revelation 11:15-17). Note, "Grace to you and peace, from Him who is and who was and who is to come . . . ." (Rev. 1:4) and "We give You thanks O Lord, the Almighty, who are and who were." (Rev. 11:17). At the start of Revelation Christ is yet to come, "John to the seven churches that are in Asia: grace and peace, from Him who is and who was and who is to come." (Rev. 1:4) And again, "And the four living creatures, each one having six wings, are full of eyes around and within; and day and night they do not cease to say, "holy, holy, holy is the Lord God, the Almighty, who was and who is and who is to come."" (Rev. 4:8). Now He has come, the phrase "who is to come" has been omitted. "We give thanks O Lord God, the Almighty, who are and who were . . ." Christ has come to usher in His kingdom at the sound of the seventh trumpet. "In a moment, in the twinkling of an eye, at the last trumpet; for the trumpet will sound, and the dead will be raised imperishable, and we will be changed." (1 Cor. 15:52). "For the Lord Himself will descend from heaven with a shout, with the voice of the archangel and with the trumpet of God, and the dead in Christ will rise first. Then we who are alive and remain will be caught up together with them in the clouds to meet the Lord in the air, and so we shall always be with the Lord." (1 Thess. 4:16-17). At the sound of the last trumpet the Lord will return to gather His elect and establish His kingdom.

Who is currently the ruler of the world? "Our struggle is not against flesh and blood, but against the rulers, against the powers, against the world forces of this darkness, against the spiritual forces of wickedness in the heavenly places." (Eph. 6:12). "We know that we are of God, and that the whole world lies in the power of the Evil One." (1 John 5:19). The current ruler of this world is Satan. But at the sound of the last trumpet the kingdom of the world becomes the kingdom of Christ. Satan loses all his power and authority. He can no longer deceive the saints as they have been removed from the world. There is no longer any influence in the world by the Holy Spirit as the Holy Spirit has been removed from the earth. The only thing to remain on the earth is Satan and His followers. The third and final woe for the earth is that nothing will restrain evil and that God will pour out His wrath upon the earth until the final destruction. Satan sees his world crumble before him and there is nothing he can do about it. The twenty four elders praise God because He has taken all control from Satan and has begun to reign on earth. Up to this time God allowed Satan to rule the earth but now God has taken charge and is now fully and completely in charge of the events to follow.

"And the nations were enraged, and Your wrath came, and the time came for the dead to be judged, and the time to reward Your bond-servants the prophets and the saints and those who fear Your name, the small and the great, and to destroy those who destroy the earth. And the temple of God which is in heaven was opened; and the ark of His covenant appeared in His temple, and there were flashes of lightening and sounds and peals of thunder and an earthquake and a great hailstorm." (Rev. 11:18). These are the events to follow. The nations are enraged. There is no peace to be found anywhere. Everyone is angry with everyone else. The wrath of God is poured out on the earth. The spiritually dead will be judged. The bond servants will be rewarded. And all evil will be destroyed. We will see these things unfold in the following chapters of Revelation. The temple of God in heaven is opened for the saints. The temple that was rebuilt in Jerusalem has been abandoned and turned over to those who dwell on earth. The ark of the covenant now resides in the heavenly temple. And nature responds with lightening, thunder, an earthquake and hailstorm.

But, the saints have peace and contentment. They have been removed from the earth and they no longer experience the effects of sin. There will be no more suffering or pain or crying or mourning for them. They are now finally safe and secure. The martyrs who cried out, "How long, how long?!" are about to have their blood avenged. Stephen was the first Christian martyr but we can go back to the very beginning and find that Abel was killed by Cain because of his religious conviction to obey God. So Abel was the first martyr. All of the martyrs, both Old and New Testament, have been waiting for this time. And finally God is about to set things straight.

Questions Chapter 11

Read Revelation 11

Read Revelation 11:1-2

    1.   What three things was John told to measure?

Read Ezekiel 44:15-19

    2.   What do we learn about the temple, inner court, and outer court?

    3.   Who is allowed in the inner court?

Read Revelation 1:6; 5:10; and 20:6

    4.   Who will be allowed in the inner court of this temple?

    5.   What will happen in the outer court?

    6.   When will the happen?

    7.   What is the temple?

Read Revelation 11:3-14 Two Witnesses

    8.   What will the two witnesses prophecy about?

    9.   How long will they prophecy?

10. How will they be clothed?

11. What is the meaning of sack cloth? Genesis 37:34;

Read 1 Kings 21:25-28

12. What was the result of Ahab's mourning?

13. What are the two witnesses mourning over?

14. How are the two witnesses described? See Revelation 11:4

15. In what way do you think that the witnesses are lamp stands?

16. What is the significance of the olive trees? See Psalm 52; Zechariah 4:12-14

17. From your earlier study what did you find that the lamp stand represents?

It is unlikely that the two witnesses are two churches. However could it be that the two witnesses, like the church, carry the light into the world?

18. Who are the two witnesses?

19. What do the following say concerning witnesses?

    Deuteronomy 19:15

    Deuteronomy 31:26

Luke 24:44

John 1:45

Acts 28:23

Romans 3:21

The two witnesses are not identified and may be anybody, however, consider the following:

20. Who was with Jesus at the transfiguration ? Luke 9:28

21. What did Elijah do according to James 5:17-18

22. How does this compare to Revelation 11: 6?

23. What did Moses do according to Exodus 7:19 and Exodus 8, 9, 10?

24. How does this compare to Revelation 11:6?

25. We cannot say for sure but could it be that the two witnesses are Moses and Elijah?

Read Revelation 11:7

26. Where does the Beast come from?

27. When does he show up?

28. Where is it on our timeline?

29. What do we learn from the following:

Revelation 9:11; Who is the angel of the Abyss?

Revelation 13:1-10; Who do you think this Beast is?

Revelation 13:11-18; Who do you think this Beast is?

Revelation 17:6-8; Who do you think this Beast is?

Revelation 11:7; Who do you think this Beast is?

Read Revelation 11:7-14

30. In what city were the two witnesses killed?

31. Why do you think it is figuratively called Sodom and Egypt?

32. Who will look at the dead bodies of the witnesses?

33. What will their reaction be to the dead witnesses?

34. How long did they lie in the streets?

35. What happened to them?

36. What was the peoples reaction to their resurrection?

This completes the second woe

37. What comes next?

CHAPTER 12

The Woman, The Dragon, The Child, and The Angel

Read Chapter 12 of Revelation

Two signs are presented in this chapter; the woman and the Dragon. They are called signs because they are something that give direction or point to something else. Though these signs are separate, they are related and are about the same events. The first sign is about Israel and its struggles, from the establishment of the nation of Israel to the birth of Jesus, as they wait for the promised Messiah. (Rev. 12:1-2). The sign continues after the birth of Jesus through and up to the blowing of the last trumpet. (Rev.12:5-6). The second sign is about Satan and his authority on the earth as he waits to destroy the coming Messiah. (Rev. 12:3-4). This sign continues, with Satan being thrown out of heaven and his failure on earth to win over the saints. (Rev. 12:7-17). There are many signs in the Bible. "Then God said, "Let there be lights in the expanse of the heavens to separate the day from the night, and let them be for signs and seasons and for days and for years." (Gen. 1:14). The lights in the heavens; the sun, the moon, the stars are signs that show us when we can expect the seasons to change or the day to turn dark and they provide a means of counting days, and months and years. "God said, "This is the sign of the covenant which I am making between Me and you and every living creature that is with you, for all successive generations; I set My bow in the cloud, and it shall be for a sign of a covenant between Me and the earth."" (Gen. 9:12-

13). The rainbow is a sign, even today, that tells us that God will never again entirely destroy the earth with a flood. Every time we see a rainbow we should be reminded of God's covenant with us. "All the people kept silent, and were listening to Barnabas and Paul as they were relating what signs and wonders God had done through them among the Gentiles." (Acts 15:12). The many miracles of God are not just supernatural events that God causes to happen. They are signs that show us the great power and mercy of God. The two signs in this chapter of Revelation are not to be interpreted literally. They are to be understood as signs that point to or show us some greater truth. The events revealed by the two signs do not follow the events we have covered so far. The signs cover a period of time beginning with the establishment of Israel through the great tribulation.

"A great sign appeared in heaven: a woman clothed with the sun, and the moon under her feet, and on her head a crown of twelve stars; and she was with child; and she cried out, being in labor and in pain to give birth." (Rev. 12:1-2). We can only interpret this passage in light of what other Scripture tells us. "Now he (Joseph) had another dream, and related it to his brothers, and said, "Lo, I have had still another dream; and behold, the sun and the moon and eleven stars were bowing down to me." He related it to his father and to his brothers; and his father rebuked him and said to him, "What is this dream that you have had? Shall I and your mother and your brothers actually come to bow ourselves down before you to the ground?"" (Gen. 37:9-10). Joseph's dream is interpreted by his father. The stars are Joseph's brothers, the sun is Jacob and the moon is Rachel. Looking further into Scripture, "The Lord announces, "Israel burned incense to the gods that were named after Baal. I will punish her for all of the times she did that. She decorated herself with rings and jewelry. Then she went after her lovers. But she forgot all about me. "So now I am going to draw her back to me. I will lead her into the desert. There I will speak tenderly to her. I will give her back her vineyards. I will make the Valley of Achor a door of hope for her. Then she will love me, as she did when she was young. She will love me just as she did when she came up out of Egypt. "A new day is coming," announces the Lord. "Israel will call me My Husband. She will no longer call me My Master. She will no longer speak about the gods that are named after Baal. She will not pray to them for help anymore. At that time I will make a covenant for the good of my people. I will make it with the wild animals and the birds of the air. It will also be made with the creatures that move on the ground. I will remove bows and swords and other weapons of war from the land. Then my people can lie down in safety. I will make Israel my own. She will belong to me forever. I will do to her what is right and fair. I will love her tenderly. I will be faithful to her. And she will recognize me as the Lord." (Hosea 2:13-20). This depicts Israel as a woman and God as her husband. The reader may want to refer to Jeremiah 3:19-20, Ezekiel 16:8-14, and Isaiah 54:1-7. Scripture often depicts Israel as a woman. Based on the above we can now understand Revelation 12:1-2 "A great sign appeared in heaven: a woman clothed with the sun, and the moon under her feet, and on her head a crown of twelve stars; and she was with child; and she cried out, being in labor and in pain to give birth." The woman is Israel, the sun is Jacob, the moon is Rachel, the twelve stars are the twelve sons of Jacob or twelve tribes of Israel. What about the child? All of Israel was looking forward to the coming of the Messiah. Daniel writes, "so you are to know and discern that from the issuing of the decree to restore and rebuild Jerusalem until Messiah the Prince there will be seven weeks and sixty two weeks." (Daniel 9:26). Daniel prophesies the coming of Jesus to the very day. Matthew writes, "The record of the genealogy of Jesus the Messiah, the son of David, the son of Abraham . . . ." (Matt. 1:1). Matthew shows the Messiah to be Jesus and that His roots are found in Israel. The theme of Old Testament Scripture is that there will be a Messiah to come to redeem them. Israel waits on the coming of the Messiah as though she is in labor. As Israel is waiting for the Messiah she goes through significant pain and suffering. The reader may refer to Hebrews 11-12:6 in order to fully understand the birth pains of Israel. By faith Israel endured waiting for the Messiah to come. The first sign is about Israel and its struggles, from the establishment of the nation of Israel to the birth of Jesus, as they wait for the promised Messiah.

"Then another sign appeared in heaven: and behold, a great Red Dragon having seven heads and ten horns, and on his heads were seven diadems. And his tail swept away a third of the stars of heaven and threw them to the earth." (Rev. 12:3-4a). Here is another sign. Who is the Dragon? "And the great Dragon was thrown down, the serpent of old who is called the Devil and Satan . . ." (Rev. 12:9). The Dragon is Satan. The Dragon is described as having seven heads with seven diadems. In chapter 17 of Revelation the Beast or Dragon is further described. "Here is the mind that has wisdom. The seven heads are seven mountains on which the woman sits, and they are seven kings; five have fallen, one is, and one is yet to come." (Rev. 17:9). The seven heads of the Dragon are seven world powers. "The ten horns which you saw are ten kings who have not yet received a kingdom but they receive authority as kings with the Beast for one hour." (Rev. 17:12). The ten horns of Revelation 12:3 are ten kings. The seven heads and ten horns will be discussed in detail when we get to chapter 17. For now it is sufficient to understand that the Dragon is Satan and he is shown as being the head of all the great world powers. "We know that we are of God, and that the whole world lies in the power of the Evil One." (1 John 5:19).

How is it that the Dragon's tail sweeps away a third of the stars of heaven? "As for the seven stars you saw in My right hand . . . . the seven stars are the angels of the seven churches." (Rev. 1:20). In chapter 1 of Revelation stars have been identified as angels. The stars referred to here are angels that Satan deceived into following him. They are Satan's angels. This is further explained in this chapter, "And there was war in heaven, Michael and his angels waging war with the Dragon. The Dragon and his angels waged war, and they were not strong enough, and there was no longer a place found for them in heaven. And the great Dragon was thrown down, the serpent of old who is called the Devil and Satan, who deceives the whole world; he was thrown down to the earth, and his angels were thrown down with him." (Rev. 12:7-9). Hence the Dragon's tail swept away a third of the stars, Satan's angels.

"And the Dragon stood before the woman who was about to give birth, so that when she gave birth he might devour her child. And she gave birth to a son, a male child, who is to rule all the nations with a rod of iron; and her child was caught up to God and to His throne." (Rev. 12:4b-5). The Woman is Israel, as earlier explained, and she is about to give birth to a child, Jesus. When Jesus is born Satan will do all in his power to destroy Him. "Now when they had gone, behold, an angel of the Lord appeared to Joseph in a dream and said, "Get up! Take the Child and His mother and flee to Egypt, and remain there until I tell you; for Herod is going to search for the Child to destroy Him." (Matt. 2:13). Herod, driven by Satan, attempts to destroy Jesus physically. "And He was in the wilderness forty days being tempted by Satan;" (Mark 1:13) Satan personally attempts to destroy Jesus spiritually. "Therefore, since the children share in flesh and blood, He Himself likewise also partook of the same, that through death He might render powerless him who had the power of death, that is, the Devil." (Heb. 2:14). Jesus became flesh and blood in order to fully and completely defeat Satan, the one with power over death so that we might have life eternal. Jesus defeated Satan physically, having avoided Herod's attempts on His life. Also, He defeated Satan physically as He withstood the many attempts of the Pharisees to bring Him down. He defeated him spiritually during the forty days of temptation in the wilderness as Satan tried to appeal to His humanity. And Jesus defeated Satan once and for all when He rose from the dead, taking away Satan's greatest threat to mankind, death. Satan would not be able to devour the male child, Jesus. Jesus was caught up to God and His throne when He ascended to heaven. "And after He had said these things He was lifted up while they were looking on, and a cloud received him out of their sight. (Acts 1:9).

"Then the woman fled into the wilderness where she had a place prepared by God, so that there she would be nourished for one thousand two hundred and sixty days." (Rev. 12:6). This event does not immediately follow the resurrection of Jesus. This is showing God's protection of Israel during the tribulation period, after the first trumpet blows. This will become clear as we examine the last half of the second sign (verses 7-17) where this event is given in greater detail.

"And there was war in heaven, Michael and his angels waging war with the Dragon. The Dragon and his angels waged war, and they were not strong enough, and there was no longer a place found for them in heaven. And the great Dragon was thrown down, the serpent of old, who is called the Devil and Satan, who deceives the whole world; he was thrown down to the earth, and his angels were thrown down with him. Then I heard a loud voice in heaven saying, "Now the salvation, and the power, and the kingdom of our God and the authority of His Christ have come, for the accuser of our brethren has been thrown down, he who accuses them before our God day and night. And they overcame him because of the blood of the Lamb and because of the word of their testimony, and they did not love their life even when faced with death. For this reason rejoice, O heavens and you who dwell in them. Woe to the earth and the sea, because the Devil has come down to you, having great wrath, knowing that he has only a short time. And when the Dragon saw that he was thrown down to the earth, he persecuted the woman who gave birth to the male child. But the two wings of the great eagle were given to the woman, so that she could fly into the wilderness to her place, where she was nourished for a time, times, and half a time, from the presence of the serpent. And the serpent poured water like a river out of his mouth after the woman, so he might cause her to be swept away with the flood. But the earth helped the woman, and the earth opened its mouth and drank up the river which the Dragon poured out of its mouth. So the Dragon was enraged with the woman, and went off to make war with the rest of her children, who keep the commandments of God and hold to the testimony of Jesus." (Rev. 12:7-17).

Referring back to our time line presented in chapter seven:

/seven seals/seven trumpets/pouring out of seven bowls of wrath/
1260 days   1260 days   30 days

(See full time line in the appendix)

The duration from the arrival of the Antichrist to the end of God's wrath is 2550 days. As shown earlier in Chapter 7 the seventieth week of Daniel includes the time of the seals and the time of the trumpets, 2520 days. Satan makes a firm covenant with Israel for these seven years. He promises peace and arranges for the temple to be rebuilt. In the middle of the week he declares himself to be God and puts a stop to sacrifices and grain offerings and begins to bring destruction.

Perhaps it would be good to explain the nature and character of Satan. Satan is a complete opposite of God. God is Father, Son, and Holy Spirit. Satan is father, son, and evil spirit. God, the Father, is creator and supreme over all things. He is truth and righteousness. Satan is destructor and subject to God in all things. He is a liar and unable to be righteous in anything. God, the Son, is Redeemer and Savior. He came in the flesh, lived among us, taught us all truth, died, rose from the dead in three days, and secured eternal life for those who believe in Him. Satan, the Antichrist, the son, is condemner and destroyer. He will come in the flesh and live among us. He will deceive all those he can. He will die and be resurrected and secure eternal death for all those who believe in him. God, the Holy Spirit, is our comforter and convicts us to the way of truth. He guides believers throughout their life and delivers them to life. Satan, the False Prophet, the evil spirit, is our tormentor and attempts to lead as many as he can to follow Satan. He guides unbelievers throughout their lives and delivers them to destruction.

The Antichrist will be Satan come to earth in the flesh to make his final attempt to take over the world. He will come into power when he brings peace to Israel and arranges for the temple to be rebuilt. After three and a half years things change. There is war in heaven and Satan is thrown down to earth along with his angels. The Antichrist will be killed but he will be resurrected. "I saw one of his heads as if it had been slain, and his fatal wound was healed. And the whole earth was amazed and followed after the Beast." (Rev. 13:3). His true nature will be revealed as he viciously goes after the Jews but they flee to a place God has provided for them and God provides special protection for them. Satan then turns his attack on Gentile believers with an even greater fury. Satan knows he has little time now and must exert every effort he can to win the world. Although there will be perilous and difficult times ahead, there is also an advantage for God's people. The accuser no longer has an audience before God. There is no one to accuse and condemn people before God. Those who accept and have accepted Christ as their Savior will be strong and able to endure the times ahead, remaining faithful even to death. But the earth and those who dwell in it, the unsaved, will be in for extreme torment.

Questions Chapter 12

Read Revelation 12

1. How many signs are there?

2. Read the following. And see how the Word sign is used.

   Genesis 1:14

   Genesis 9:12

   Exodus 4:17

   Exodus 31:16-18

   Psalm 65:8

   Isaiah 7:14

   Matthew 12:38

   Luke 11:16

   Acts 15:12

   Romans 4:11

   1 Corinthians 14:20-25

3. Based on what you read what do you think a sign is?

Can you see that a sign is something that points to something else? The sign itself is not important. What is important is the thing that the sign points to.

4. How do you interpret the sign of Revelation 12:1-2?

Read Genesis 37:9-10

5. What are the stars, the sun and the moon?

Read Isaiah 54:1-7

6. What or who is this about? How does this depict Israel?

Read Jeremiah 3:19-20

7. What or who is this about? How does this depict Israel?

Read Ezekiel 16:8-14

8. What or who is this about? How does this depict Israel?

Read Hosea 2:14-20

9. What or who is this about? How does this depict Israel?

10. In what way have we seen Israel cry out in labor and in pain to give birth?

Israel suffered much trials and tribulations and pain over the course of time waiting on the Messiah.

11. What are some of those ways?

Read Hebrews chapter 11- 12:11

> 12. In light of what you have read does Hebrews 12:11 have a relationship to Revelation 12:2?

> 13. In Revelation 12:2 who is it that the woman is going to give birth to?

Read Revelation 12:3 This is another sign.

> 14. Who is the Dragon? See verse 9

Read Revelation 17:8-13 Beast with seven heads described.

> 15. Is this the same Beast?

> 16. What do the seven heads in Revelation 17:9-11 represent?

> 17. What is represented by the ten horns?

Read Revelation 1:20

> 18. Who or what are the stars?

Read Revelation 12:4, 7-9

> 19. In light of 7-9 who or what are the stars in verse 4?

> 20. What is the Dragon doing in Revelation 12:4?

Read Job 1:7

    21. What is Satan doing?

    22. At the time of Job was Satan free to roam the earth and to appear in heaven?

Read Zechariah 3:1-2

    23. What is Satan doing?

    24. Where is Satan?

At the time of Joshua the high priest Satan is acting as the accuser.

    25. Where is the Dragon (Satan) in Revelation 12:4?

Read Revelation 12:5

    26. Who is the child?

    27. When was He caught up to God and His throne?

Read Revelation 12:6

    28. How long would the woman be protected?

    29. When would this protection start?

Read Revelation 12:7-11

    30. When does this happen? See Revelation 12:14

31. How did the brethren overcome Satan? See Revelation12:11

Read Revelation12:12

32. How long does the Devil have?

33. What do you think life would be like under the rule of the revealed Antichrist?

Read Revelation 12:13

34. Who will the Antichrist first focus his attention on when he reveals himself?

Read Revelation 12:14-16

35. Will the Antichrist succeed in his attacks on Israel?

Read Revelation 12:17

36. When his efforts to attack Israel fail who will the Antichrist turn to?

37. What can we do to protect ourselves from him?

CHAPTER 13

Two Beasts

Read Chapter 13 of Revelation

Chapter 13 introduces the Beast from the Sea and the Beast from the Earth. There are three players in this chapter; the Dragon, the Beast from the Sea, and the Beast from the Earth. Each of these has a specific role to play.

In the end, "The Beast was seized and with him the False Prophet . . . ; these were thrown into the lake of fire . . . " (Rev.19:20). And, "the Devil who deceived them was thrown into the lake of fire and brimstone, where the Beast and the False Prophet are also." (Rev. 20:10). Clearly there are three entities; the Devil, the Beast, and the False Prophet. Further in 1 John 2:22 we read, "Who is the liar but the one who denies that Jesus is the Christ? This is the Antichrist, the one who denies the Father and the Son." The term Antichrist is only used four times in Scripture; 1 John 2:18, 1 John 2:22, 1 John 4:3, and 2 John 1:7. John uses this term in a general sense to describe any who deny Christ and do not acknowledge that He has come in the flesh. In 1 John 2:18 John writes, "Children, it is the last hour; and just as you heard that Antichrist is coming, even now many antichrists have appeared; from this we know that it is the last hour." It appears that John is expecting that the Antichrist is about to come and that until that time many antichrist types will appear.

In our previous chapter we showed that there is a triune Devil just as there is a triune God. This chapter gives us considerable detail concerning their relationship to one another. "And the Dragon stood on the sand of the seashore." (Revelation 13:1a). The Dragon is the father counterpart of the Devil or the first person of Satan. This will shortly become obvious.

THE BEAST OF THE SEA

"Then I saw a Beast coming up out of the sea, having ten horns and seven heads, and on his horns were blasphemous names. And the Beast which I saw was like a leopard, and his feet were like those of a bear, and his mouth like the mouth of a lion." (Rev. 13:1b-2). "Why do you wonder? I will tell you the mystery of the Beast that carries her which has seven heads and ten horns . . . . Here is the mind that has wisdom. The seven heads are seven mountains on which the woman sits, and they are seven kings; five have fallen, one is, and one is yet to come." (Rev. 17:7, 9, 10). "The ten horns are ten kings which have not yet received a kingdom." (Rev. 17:12). The Beast of the Sea is the same Beast as the scarlet Beast in Revelation 17. The seven heads are seven world empires which the Beast has authority over. Six of these empires have already appeared, five before John's day, one during his days and there is now one yet to come. Remember that for now Satan is the ruler of the world. The ten horns are ten kings who have yet to receive their power. We will explore them in more detail in chapter 17. The Beast is described as being like a leopard with feet like a bear and the mouth of a lion. God uses these terms to describe how he responds to Israel when they have become complacent, forgetting God and turning to idols. "So I will be like a lion to them; like a leopard I will lie in wait by the hillside. I will encounter them like a bear robbed of her cubs, and I will tear open their chests; there I will also devour them like a lioness, as a wild Beast would tear them." (Hosea 13:7-8). These characteristics are now applied to the Beast of the Sea. The Beast will be like a leopard, lying in wait for its prey. It will sneak around and hide until the last moment when it strikes out to capture its' prey. By then it will be too late. The leopard relies on its' cunning soft quiet approach to catch its' prey off guard and then strikes. The bear is a ferocious beast especially when his young are threatened. The bear will not easily give up and turn away. He is relentless in his attacks stopping at nothing until he has won his victory. The Beast described here in Revelation 13 is also relentless. He becomes violent and aggressive when his territory is threatened. He refuses to give in even a little. And when he has pounced upon his prey he devours it like a lion, leaving nothing behind. He sits with great pride over those he has brought to ruin. His character is to be feared more than anything else on earth. Only God can protect us from one such as this.

" And the Dragon gave him his power and his throne and great authority." (Rev. 13:2). The Beast of the Sea gets his power, throne, and authority from the Dragon, or Satan. This is the Antichrist. This is Satan come to earth to rule the world. He is the second person of the Satan. When Jesus walked on this earth He had the power, throne and authority of God. "So Jesus said, "When you lift up the Son of Man then you will know that I am He, and I do nothing on My own initiative, but I speak these things as the Father taught Me." (John 8:28). Jesus says He does nothing on His own initiative. Everything He does proceeds from the Father. The Beast from the Sea, the Antichrist, does nothing on his own but gets his power, throne, and authority from Satan.

"I saw one of his heads as if it had been slain, and his fatal wound was healed. And the whole earth was amazed and followed after the Beast; they worshipped the Dragon because he gave his authority to the Beast; and they worshipped the Beast saying, "Who is like the Beast, and who is able to wage war with him?" There was given to him a mouth speaking arrogant Words and blasphemies, and authority to act for forty-two months was given to him. And he opened his mouth in blasphemies against God, to blaspheme His name and His tabernacle, that is those who dwell in heaven." (Rev. 13:3-6). This was prophesied very early in Scripture. God cursed the serpent because he had deceived Eve in the Garden. "And I will put enmity between you and the woman, and between your seed and her seed; He shall bruise you on the head and you shall bruise Him on the heel." (Gen. 3:16 NASB). The Antichrist has a fatal wound on his head. Fatal wound does not mean a wound capable of causing death it means a wound that does in fact cause death. The Antichrist has been slain. But his fatal wound has been healed. He has been resurrected. In chapter 7 we showed how the seventy weeks of Daniel 9 had already been fulfilled. But we also showed how the seventieth week in Daniel 9 is a prophecy concerning the end times and gives us a time sequence of events relating to this time. "He will make a firm covenant for many for one week, but in the middle of the week he will put a stop to sacrifice and grain offering; on the wing of abominations will come one who makes desolate, even until a complete destruction." (Dan. 9:27). At the beginning of the tribulation period, with the opening of the first seal, the Antichrist appears riding a white horse. Now, in the middle of the week, after three and a half years, the Antichrist reveals himself. During the first three and a half years the Antichrist has brought peace to Israel and arranged for them to be able to rebuild the temple in Jerusalem. There will be wars and famines during this time and many will die. But people will see the Antichrist as a good person, working to help Israel get through these difficult times. Now, in the middle of the week he will be killed. The text says, "I saw one of his heads as if it had been slain." Now there are seven heads, representing seven world powers. In the days of John, five had previously been in power, one was currently in power and one was to come to power. We are now seeing the seventh head that has come to power and has now been slain. He is resurrected and the whole world is amazed. This coincides with the blowing of the first trumpet.

/ seven seals/ seven trumpets/pouring out of seven bowls of wrath/
1260 days   1260 days   30 days
Antichrist arrives Antichrist revealed

(See full time line in the appendix)

The Antichrist has come out and denies God and the power of God, he himself claiming to be god. He stops the sacrifice and demands that he be worshipped. "Many will be purged, purified and refined, but the wicked will act wickedly; and none of the wicked will understand, but those who have insight will understand. From the time the regular sacrifice is abolished and the abomination of desolation is set up, there will be 1290 days." (Dan. 12:10-11). The abomination of desolation is the Antichrist sitting on the throne in the temple of God saying, "Worship me, I am invincible, I was killed but yet I live! God has done nothing to save and protect you during this time but look at what I have done! All those who worship God are fools!"

"It was also given to him to make war with the saints and to overcome them, and authority over every tribe and people and tongue and nation was given to him. All who dwell on the earth will worship him, everyone whose name has not been written from the foundation of the world in the book of life of the Lamb who has been slain. If anyone has an ear let him hear. If anyone is destined for captivity, to captivity he goes; if anyone kills with the sword, with the sword he must be killed. Here is the perseverance of the faith of the saints." (Rev. 13:7-10). There will be great persecution for the saints during this time. The Antichrist will have authority over all things and he will come after those who refuse to worship him. But only those who dwell on the earth (the unsaved) will worship him. Everyone will not understand, only those who have ears, only those who accept and believe the Word of God. The saints will persevere through this time. It does not matter if one is imprisoned or if one is killed. God has a reward so grand that Satan cannot deceive or turn away God's people. He cannot wrench them out of God's hand. Those who keep the faith will reap their reward. "For I am convinced that neither death nor life, nor angels, nor principalities, nor things present, nor things to come, nor powers nor height, nor depth, nor any other created thing, will be able to separate us from the love of God which is in Christ Jesus." (Rom. 8:38-39). "Those who persevere bear fruit." (Luke 8:15). "Those who persevere do good and seek for glory and honor and immortality, eternal life. (Rom. 2:7). "Tribulations bring about perseverance, perseverance proven character, proven character hope, hope does not disappoint because we have the love of God in our hearts." (Rom. 5:3-5). It does not matter what the Antichrist says or does, we remain safe and secure in the loving hands of God our Savior.

THE BEAST of the EARTH

"Then I saw another Beast coming up out of the earth; and he had two horns like a lamb and he spoke as a Dragon." (Rev, 13:11). This is the third person of Satan. There is the father, Satan; the son, the Antichrist; and the evil spirit, False Prophet. A prophet is one who speaks for God and seeks to turn people to follow God. A false prophet is one who speaks for Satan and tries to turn people to follow Satan. The appearance of the False Prophet is one like a lamb. He appears to be gentle and peaceful. But when he speaks he speaks like a Dragon. His Words are the Words of Satan. He is a wolf in sheep's clothing.

"He exercises all the authority of the first Beast in his presence. And he makes the earth and those who dwell in it to worship the first Beast, whose fatal wound has been healed." (Rev. 13:12). The fatal wound has been healed. The fatal wound of the Antichrist brought death to the Antichrist. But now the wound is healed. The Antichrist has risen from the dead. The primary purpose of the False Prophet is to turn the people away from God and towards the Antichrist. There are many people in the church who claim to be Christians yet they do not have their dwelling in heaven. They dwell on earth and follow after the Antichrist worshipping the first Beast. Some of these do not have their names be written in the Lamb's book of life. They will continue to follow the Antichrist until they die and reap their just reward. However, those whose names are in the book of life will see the light and turn away from the Antichrist and follow after Jesus. These will have their dwelling in heaven. The False Prophet is proclaiming the Antichrist to be the savior of the world and pointing to his resurrection as proof that he is worthy to be worshipped.

"He performs great signs, so that he even makes fire come down out of heaven to the earth in the presence of men. And he deceives those who dwell on earth because of the signs which it was given to him to perform in the presence of the Beast, telling those who dwell on the earth to make an image to the Beast who had the wound of the sword and has come to life. And it was given to him to give breath to the image of the Beast, so that the image of the Beast would even speak and cause as many as do not worship the image of the Beast to be killed." (Rev. 13:13-15). The False Prophet is capable of performing miracles and wonders. "False christs and false prophets will arise and show great signs and wonders so as to mislead, if possible, even the elect." Matt. 24:23-25). Jesus told us this would happen. The False Prophet will give his every effort to mislead the people. He will diligently seek to change the elect. But this is not possible as their names have been recorded in the book of life from the beginning of creation. Not only does the False Prophet get people to worship the Antichrist but he also convinces them to build an image of the False Prophet and he gives the image breath and a voice. We can easily understand the possibility of this with today's technology. Once the image has been created he has them worship the image. It seems inconceivable that anyone would fall for this today. Why would anyone worship an object made by man? Man today is far too wise for this foolishness. However, "God will send among them a deluding influence so that they will believe what is false." (2 Thess. 2:11). Those who dwell on earth will be deceived into worshipping the image of the Beast.

The final days are fast approaching. It is time to choose between God and Satan. No more sitting on the fence. Many of those who refuse to worship the Antichrist and the image of the Antichrist will be killed and counted among the martyrs. It is impossible for a true Christian to deny God and worship Satan. Somehow, some Christians will survive until Christ comes again at the sound of the last trumpet. These will be taken up to Jesus on a cloud. It is certainly difficult to say which is better; to live under the persecution and the effects of the great tribulation until Christ comes and we can join Him in the air or to go ahead and be killed by the False Prophet and be immediately with Christ in heaven watching all these events take place. The rest will fall prey to the hands of the False Prophet and will worship the Beast.

"And he causes all the small and the great, and the rich and the poor, and the free men and the slaves, to be given a mark on their right hand or on their forehead, and he provides that no one will be able to buy or sell, except the one who has the mark, either the name of the Beast or the number of his name." (Rev. 13:16-17a). This is the last and most damaging thing the Antichrist does. He demands that everyone take a stand. You are on his side or you are against him. Life will be extremely difficult for those who choose to go against the Antichrist. They will not be able to buy or sell anything. How long can people sustain themselves if they need to be self sufficient? Perhaps one could put away a large storehouse of goods to help them through this time. But to do this you must be prepared. We must know that when the Antichrist first appears we will need to start storing up supplies. From the building of the temple we will have three and a half years. When the decree is issued it will be too late. And then, once you have your supplies in place and the decree is issued you must protect what you have. You must protect what you have from those who have no moral or ethical values and will take whatever they can get by force, but you must also wrestle with a greater issue. Can you deny your precious goods that you have put away to other Christians, your neighbors, your friends, and your family who either failed to prepare or have not put away enough to last them through the times?

Is it really that bad to go ahead and get the mark? What if you are really, really hungry? What if you really need to go to a doctor? What if your child needs food? "If anyone worships the Beast and his image, and receives a mark on his forehead or on his hand, he also will drink of the wine of the wrath of God, which is mixed in full strength, in the cup of His anger; and he will be tormented with fire and brimstone in the presence of the holy angels and in the presence of the Lamb." (Rev. 14:9-10). Yes, it really is that bad. There are no exceptions. It matters not what your situation is. It would be better to die of starvation than to experience the full wrath of God.

"Here is wisdom. Let him who has understanding calculate the number of the Beast, for the number is that of a man; and his number is six hundred and sixty-six." (Rev. 13:17b). For this I refer to, "The secrete things belong to the LORD our God but the things revealed belong to us and our sons forever, that we may observe all the Words of this law." (Deut. 29:29). There are some things that have not yet been revealed. We can speculate on what they may be but we are only fooling ourselves. A time will come when it will be evident what the number of the Beast means. Until that time we must be content to simply accept that the Beast is a real being, that he will be identifiable, and that we will know him by his name.

Though we do not know for sure what the number 666 means I offer the following as speculation. The number seven is the number of perfection or completion. The number seven, seven, seven represents God. God is perfect and holy without sin or blemish. God is a triune God; God the Father, God the Son, and God the Holy Spirit. Each of the persons of God is perfect and holy and just. They are all perfect sevens thus seven, seven, seven represents the triune God in perfection and holiness. Conversely to this, six is a number of incompletion and imperfection. The number six represents man because he is imperfect, sinful, and no good. Satan's number is the number of man; six, six, six. This represents the total state of imperfection of Satan. Satan is a triune being; Satan, the Antichrist, and the False Prophet. The number six, six, six represents the full imperfection of each of the persons of Satan. Even so there appears to be more to this than we are able to determine at this time. When the Antichrist is revealed we will then understand how the number six, six, six truly identifies Satan.

Questions Chapter 13

Read revelation 13

1. Who are the players?

   Who is the Dragon?

   Who is the Beast from the sea?

   Who is the Beast from the land?

   BEAST FROM THE SEA

Read Revelation 13:1-10

2. What does Revelation 13:1 say about the beast from the sea?

3. Compare this to the Red Dragon of Revelation 12:3 Does this sound like the same beast?

Read Revelation 17:7-13

4. Does this sound like the same beast?

5. What are the Seven heads?

6. What are the 10 horns?

7. What does Revelation 13: 2 say about the beast?

8. What characteristics of a leopard could be applied to the Antichrist? See Hosea 13:7

9. In what way could the Antichrist be said to have feet like a bear?

10. In what way do you think the Antichrist could be said to have the mouth of a lion?

11. From where does the Antichrist get his power, throne and authority?

Read John 5:19, 30

12. Where does Jesus get his power, throne and authority from?

Read Revelation 13:3-4. Compare to Genesis 3:15

13. What is this a picture of?

14. Why did people worship the Dragon?

15. Why did they worship the Antichrist?

Read Revelation 13:5

16. How long would the Antichrist be in power?

Read Revelation 13:6

17. Who does the Antichrist attack?

Remember our study on those who dwell in heaven and those who dwell on earth

Read Revelation 13:7

    18. Who does the Antichrist attack?

Read Revelation 13:8

    19. Who will worship the Antichrist?

Read Revelation 13:9

    20. Are we to understand this?

Read Revelation 13:10

    21. What do the following have in common with verse 10?

        Jeremiah 15:2

        Jeremiah 43:11

        Genesis 9:6

        Matthew 26:52

        Revelation 11:18

Read Revelation 14:12, 13

    22. What does this say about the perseverance of the saints?

23. What do the following say about perseverance?

Luke 8:15

Romans 2:7

Romans 5:3-5

Romans 8:25

BEAST FROM THE EARTH

Read Revelation 13:11-18

24. What does Revelation13:11 tell us about the Beast?

25. When one first sees this Beast what would their impression be?

26. How would that change when the Beast spoke?

Read Revelation 13:12

27. Where does this Beast get its power?

28. What is his purpose?

Read Revelation 13:13

29. What does this and the following say concerning the Beast?

2 Thessalonians 2:8-9

Matthew 24:23-25

Read Revelation 13:14-15

30. What is the goal of the Beast?

31. What do the following say about being deceived?

    1 Corinthians 6:9

    1 Corinthians 15:33

    2 Corinthians 11:3

    Galatians 6:7

    Ephesians 5:6

    2 Thessalonians 2:3

    James 1:6

    1 John 3:7

32. What do the previous passages say about our part in being deceived? Can we unknowingly be deceived?

Read Revelation 13:16-17

33. Who is forced to get the mark?

34. What will the mark allow those who receive it to do?

35. If only those who have the mark are allowed to buy or sell does this imply that there will be others who do not have the mark who will not be allowed to buy or sell?

Read Revelation 14:9-10

36. What happens to those who get the mark?

Read Revelation 13:18

37. What is the number of the Beast?

38. What do you think it means?

777 is perfection and is God's number. In that God is triune in nature and the Father, Son, and Holy Spirit are all perfect 7s.

666 is mans number. Man is born in sin and can do no good. Satan is triune in nature and Satan, the Antichrist, and the False Prophet are all 6's and full of sin and can do no good.

CHAPTER 14

Angels

Read Chapter 14 of Revelation

*C*hapter 14 describes five separate events. There is not a time sequence to these events but they all occur just before or just after the last trumpet. It is as though John was in a theater and before him there appeared five scenes giving further detail to the last call to redemption. There seems to be a sense of urgency as the angels proclaim the gospel one last time. First of all, there are 144,000 on Mount Zion, before the throne. This scene is just after the last trumpet as the 144,000 have been taken up to heaven. Secondly, there is an angel proclaiming the gospel throughout all the earth. This happens just before the last trumpet as a final call to redemption. The third thing is the proclamation that Babylon has fallen. The fourth thing is a warning for those who worship the Beast and receive his mark. This, too, happens just before the last trumpet as a final plea to accept Christ and be saved. And the last thing is the reapers. First the reapers reap the saved at the last trumpet and then the unsaved are reaped after the last bowl of wrath. All of these events urgently proclaim the message, "Repent and be saved! The end is near!"

SCENE 1

"Then I looked and behold, the Lamb was standing on Mount Zion, and with Him one hundred and forty-four thousand, having His name and the name of His Father written on their foreheads. And I heard a voice from heaven, like the sound of many waters and like the sound of loud thunder, and the voice which I heard was like the sound of harpist playing on their harps. And they sang a new song before the throne and before the four living creatures and the elders; and no one could learn the song except the one hundred and forty-four thousand who had been purchased from the earth. These are the ones who have not been defiled with women, for they have kept themselves chaste. These are the ones who follow the Lamb wherever He goes. These have been purchased from among men as first fruits to God and to the Lamb. And no lie was found in their mouth; and they are blameless." (Rev. 14:1-5).

These are the one hundred and forty-four thousand that we read about earlier in Chapter 7 of Revelation. Before the first trumpet they were given the mark of God on their foreheads in order to protect them from the coming events of the seven trumpets. In Chapter 7 it only says that they were sealed on their foreheads. Now we know that the seal that was put on them was the name of Jesus and His Father. This was not some mystical seal. It would be evident to all who see them that they belong to God. These are off limits to Satan and his angels. These same ones now stand before the throne of God. They have been carried up to heaven. They have experienced the events of the seven trumpets. Although they were protected from harm during this time, they were there, they were witnessing, and they saw what was happening.

And now they stand before the throne singing praises to God. They sing a new song that no one can learn but them. Here again we refer to Deuteronomy 29:29, "The secret things belong to the LORD our God, but the things revealed belong to us and to our sons forever." We just don't know what is so special about the song they were singing or why no one else could learn to sing it. But what it does point out is that these one hundred and forty-four thousand are very special in the sight of God.

They have not defiled themselves with women. Paul tells us in 1 Corinthians Chapter 7 that a married man is distracted by having the responsibility of taking care of his wife. "One who is unmarried is concerned about the things of the Lord, how he may please the Lord; but one who is married is concerned about the things of the world, how he may please his wife, and his interests are divided." These one hundred and forty-four thousand have remained unmarried and kept themselves chaste in order to be able to devote themselves entirely to serving God. They have spent their life following Jesus and doing whatever He called them to do.

These were purchased as first fruits to God and to the Lamb. "In the exercise of His will He brought us forth by the word of truth, so that we would be a kind of first fruits among His creatures." (James 1:18). "Israel was holy to the LORD, the first of His harvest." (Jer. 2:3). The first fruit is the best of the crop. It is the cream of the crop. Israel is the first fruit of the harvest. That is, Israel is the first people God chose as His own to be holy. The rest of the nations, and people and tongues, not Israel, who have accepted Christ as their Lord and Savior, have been brought forth to be a kind of first fruits to God. So, all who profess Christ, Jew and Gentile are first fruits to God, the cream of the crop. They are perfect and holy before the Lord.

But, they were not perfect and holy in their own right; they were purchased from among men. They were purchased by the precious blood of Jesus that washes away their sin and leaves them blameless. That is, even though our Scripture says "no lie was found in their mouth and they are blameless," it does not say that they were blameless in their own right. What it says is they were "purchased from among men as first fruits." "All have turned aside, together they have become useless; there is none who does good, there is not even one." (Rom. 3:12). This statement of Paul's leaves little to be confused about. There are none who do good, period. Yet, those who accept Christ as their Lord and Savior will stand before God blameless and no lie will be found in their mouth. The blood of Jesus has cleansed them from all unrighteousness. Their sin has been completely covered and God does not see or remember any of their failings or short comings. "Blessed are those whose lawless deeds have been forgiven, and whose sins have been covered. Blessed is the man whose sin the Lord will not take into account." (Rom. 4:7).

These one hundred and forty-four thousand are special indeed. God has set them apart and even given them a special song to sing. But the good news is that we who know and love the Lord Jesus Christ will stand beside them blameless with no lie found in our mouth because we have been purchased with the precious blood of Jesus as first fruits to God.

Scene 2

"And I saw another angel flying in midheaven, having an eternal gospel to preach to those who live on the earth, and to every nation and tribe and tongue and people; and he said with a loud voice, "Fear God, and give Him glory, because the hour of His judgment has come; worship Him who made the heaven and the earth and sea and springs of waters." (Rev. 14:6-7).

The gospel being proclaimed by the angel is going out to those who live on earth and every nation, tribe and tongue. Those who live on earth are all those who still remain on the earth before the seventh trumpet sounds and before the saints are taken up to heaven. This is different than those who dwell on earth. Those who dwell on earth have their life wrapped up in earthly things. Those who live on earth find their place of abode on the earth whether they are dwelling on earth or in heaven. The gospel is proclaimed to all those who dwell on earthly things and those who dwell on heavenly things. The gospel goes out to every nation, and tribe, and tongue. No one is left out. Everyone will be assured of hearing the gospel message before the final call to repentance. They will be without excuse. Jesus says, "This gospel of the kingdom shall be preached in the whole world as a testimony to all the nations, and then the end will come." (Matt. 24:14). The end cannot come until all have heard the gospel. The gospel message of the angel is simple, Fear God and give Him glory. God is the One who created all things. Nothing was created by your hands. You have no right to glory in your own doings. The hour of judgment is here! No one will escape the scrutiny of His eyes. God will reach to the depths of your soul. All things will be revealed. Repent now and be saved! Worship God. Only He can save you from the wrath to come. No one will be able to say, "I did not know." The angel with the eternal gospel to preach will deliver his message to all those who live on earth before the last trumpet blows.

Scene 3

"And another angel, a second one, followed, saying, "Fallen, fallen is Babylon the great, she who has made all the nations drink of the wine of the passion of her immorality." (Rev. 14:8). Babylon the great has fallen. This is covered in great detail in Chapters 17 & 18. This angel follows the angel with the gospel. The message of this angel is that even as great as Babylon was it fell to ruin. The message confirms what the angel with the gospel is saying. You can bask in your own glory as Babylon did but it will only take you to destruction. The only thing you can do is to repent of your Babylonian ways and worship God. Only in God will you find your hope realized.

Scene 4

"Then another angel, a third one, followed them, saying with a loud voice, "If anyone worships the Beast and his image, and receives a mark on his forehead or on his hand, he also will drink of the wine of the wrath of God, which is mixed in full strength in the cup of His anger; and he will be tormented with fire and brimstone in the presence of the holy angels and in the presence of the Lamb. And the smoke of their torment goes up forever and ever; they have no rest day and night, those who worship the Beast and his image, and whoever receives the mark of his name." Here is the perseverance of the saints who keep the commandments of God and their faith in Jesus. And I heard a voice from heaven, saying, "Write, Blessed are the dead who die in the Lord from now on!'" "Yes," says the Spirit, "so that they may rest from their labors, for their deeds follow with them." (Rev.14:9-13).

The third angel continues with the gospel message. This time the angel gives a dire warning to those who worship the Beast. The message of the first angel was "Give glory to God and worship Him." Now the third angel is telling what the results of worshipping the Beast are. The full wrath of God is about to come upon the world. There will be no escaping it. Those who are left after the blowing of the seventh trumpet will receive the full strength of God's wrath and anger. "Then the LORD rained on Sodom and Gomorrah brimstone and fire from the LORD out of heaven." (Gen. 19:24). Once the saints have been removed from the earth what remains will be a place so full of sin, hatred, immorality, and earthly passions with nothing to restrain it that it will be like unto Sodom and Gomorrah and deserving of the same judgment. So God rains down upon the earth brimstone and fire just as He did at Sodom and Gomorrah. Ezekiel prophesies of this time, "With pestilence and with blood I will enter into judgment with him; and I will rain on him and on his troops, and on the many peoples who are with him, a torrential rain, with hailstones, fire and brimstone." (Ezek. 38:22). God's judgment will be unbearable for those who remain. The period of His wrath is but thirty days. But, His judgment will soon follow. "But for the cowardly and unbelieving and abominable and murderers and immoral persons and sorcerers and idolaters and all liars, their part will be in the lake that burns with fire and brimstone, which is the second death." (Rev. 21:8). After the judgment those who worshipped the Beast and received his mark will be thrown into the lake of fire and brimstone. From this there is no relief. The fire goes on forever and ever. There will be no rest from its torment. Twenty four hours a day, seven days a week the torment continues. The angel is proclaiming to the world that this is the last chance. Repent and be saved! Or continue to worship the Beast and partake in the full wrath of God to come. And the angel, in contrast, tells the world that there is another option to God's wrath. Those who persevere through the tribulation and refuse the mark of the Beast and refuse to worship the Beast and those who keep the commandments of God and maintain their faith in Christ Jesus will be greatly blessed and will find perfect rest from their labor and they will be rewarded for their good deeds.

Scene 5

"Then I looked, and behold, a white cloud, and sitting on the cloud was one like a son of man, having a golden crown on His head and a sharp sickle in His hand. And another angel came out of the temple, crying out with a loud voice to Him who sat on the cloud, "Put in your sickle and reap, for the hour to reap has come, because the harvest of the earth is ripe." Then He who sat on the cloud swung His sickle over the earth, and the earth was reaped." (Rev. 14:14-16). The seventh trumpet has blown. The kingdom of the earth has become the kingdom of the Lord. Those who persevered through the tribulation are taken up to meet Jesus on a cloud. "For the Lord Himself will descend from heaven with a shout, with the voice of the archangel and with the trumpet of God, and the dead in Christ will rise first. Then we who are alive and remain will be caught up together with them in the clouds to meet the Lord in the air and so we shall always be with the Lord." (1Thess. 4:16-17). This is the final gathering of the saints. This is a bodily resurrection for those who died previously. For those who are alive, they will be transformed instantaneously to immortal bodies. They have been removed from the evil forces of the earth. The effects of sin are behind them. There will be no more sorrow, or pain, or suffering, or mourning. There will be no more hatred or conflicts or war. There will be no more greed, or lust, or abuse towards our fellow man. There will be no more sickness, stress, anxiety, or death. These things will be in the past and will no longer be a part of their life or even remembered. They will reside in the safe sanctuary of Christ our Lord forever and ever.

"And another angel came out of the temple which is in heaven, and he also had a sharp sickle. Then another angel, the one who has power over fire, came out from the altar; and he called with a loud voice to him who had the sharp sickle, saying, "Put in your sharp sickle and gather the clusters from the vine of the earth, because her grapes are ripe." So the angel swung his sickle to the earth and gathered the clusters from the vine of the earth, and threw them into the great wine press of the wrath of God. And the wine press was trodden outside the city, and blood came out from the wine press, up to the horses' bridles, for a distance of two hundred miles." (Rev. 14:17-20). This is the final gathering of those who dwell on earth, the unsaved who are doomed for destruction. The first angel gathered together all the saints both living and dead for eternal life with Jesus. The second angel gathered together all the unsaved for final destruction. The number of these is beyond comprehension. The text says the number is so great that the blood from their death comes up to the horses' bridle for a distance of two hundred miles. "When the thousand years are completed, Satan will be released from his prison, and will come out to deceive the nations which are in the four corners of the earth, Gog and Magog, to gather them together for the war; the number of them is like the sand of the seashore. And they came up on the broad plain of the earth and surrounded the camp of the saints and the beloved city, and fire came down from heaven and devoured them." (Rev. 20:7-9). After the thousand year reign on earth by Christ, Satan gathers together all the unsaved and brings them in force against the saints in Jerusalem. The number of them is like the sand of the seashore. There are millions and millions of them. When they come up to the walls of Jerusalem fire comes down out of heaven and kills them and the blood from their death comes up to the horses' bridles for a distance of two hundred miles.

Building on our previous timeline or sequence chart we see the rest of the events of Revelation.

Seals / trumpets/ bowls of wrath / last bowl/Armageddon/
31/2 yrs 31/2 yrs   30 days

Millennium/ Final battle/ New Heaven-Earth
1000 yrs   Eternity

(See full time line in the appendix)

The sequence of events between the trumpets and the recreation of the New Heaven and New Earth will unfold over the next few chapters. A summary of these events is as follows. At the sound of the seventh trumpet the saints, both those dead and those alive, will be raised to meet Jesus in the air. Following their removal from the earth, God's wrath will be poured out on those who remain. After the sixth bowl of wrath, Satan will gather his army together for the battle of Armageddon. The seventh bowl of wrath is then poured out on the earth. After the seventh bowl of wrath, Jesus leads the saints on white horses against Satan and his army at Armageddon. Everyone alive on earth at the time is killed. The Antichrist and the False Prophet are thrown into the lake of fire. Satan is bound for one thousand years. Then the saints take on bodily form and reign with Christ for one thousand years. After the thousand years are completed Satan is released and the rest of the dead come to life, the unsaved. Now Satan gathers together all his followers, all the unsaved who have ever lived, and brings them to the wall outside Jerusalem to attack the saints. When they get outside the city God rains fire and brimstone down upon them and they all die. Their blood covers the horses' bridles for two hundred miles. After this Satan is thrown into the lake of fire, then the unsaved are judged and thrown into the lake of fire. The current heavens and earth are burned up with intense heat. Then a New Heaven and New Earth appear which will be our final destination. Try to keep this sequence in mind as we move forward.

QUESTIONS CHAPTER 14

Read Revelation 14

   1. What are the five parts?

Part 1

   2. What do we learn about the 144000 in Revelation 14:1, 4-5

   3. Are these the same as those sealed in Revelation 7:4?

Read Revelation 14:2,3

   4. What are the 144000 doing?

   5. Where did the 144000 come from?

Read Revelation 14:4,5

   6. How does this describe the 144000?

   7. Does Revelation 14:5 say they are blameless in their own right?

Read Hebrews 9:14, 1 Peter 1:19, and Jude 1:24

   8. How does one become blameless?

   9. What precedes Revelation 14:5?

10. If they were blameless in their own right would they need to be purchased?

11. What are the first fruits? See James 1:18, Jeremiah 2:3

Part 2

Read Revelation 14:6-7

12. What is the angel doing in verses 6 & 7?

13. What does Matthew 24:14 say?

14. What does Mark 13:10 say?

15. What is the commission of the disciples? Mark 16:15

16. Why does the angel carry the gospel to those who live on earth, to every nation, tribe, tongue and people?

Part 3

Read Revelation 14:8

17. What is the second angel doing in Revelation 14:8?

18. What is the problem with Babylon?

Part 4

Read Revelation 14:9-13

19. Will those who worship the Beast be raptured at the seventh trumpet?

Read Revelation 14:10,11.

20. How does this compare to:

Genesis 19:24

Ezekiel 38:22

Revelation 21:8

21. What will be the destiny of those who worship the Beast?

Read Revelation 14:12,13

22. What will be the destiny of those who persevere?

Part 5

Read Revelation 14:14-16

23. Who is reaped?

24. Who does the reaping?

Read Revelation 14:17-20

25. Who is reaped?

26. What happens to those reaped by the second angel?

CHAPTER 15

Another Sign

Read Chapter 15 of Revelation

Chapter 15 is another sign. This sign shows us events happening in heaven just prior to the angels pouring out the seven bowls of wrath on the earth. "Then I saw another sign in heaven, great and marvelous, seven angels who had seven plagues, which are the last, because in them the wrath of God is finished." (Rev. 15:1). We are almost to the end of time that God has allotted for the present earth. The angels will soon pour out their bowls of wrath upon the earth. This will be the last plague on the earth and it will be the worst of plagues. After the plagues there will be the battle of Armageddon and every living person that remains will be killed.

"And I saw something like a sea of glass mixed with fire, and those who had been victorious over the Beast and his image and the number of his name, standing on the sea of glass, holding harps of God. And they sang the song of Moses, the bond-servant of God, and the song of the Lamb, saying,

> "Great and marvelous are Your works,
> O Lord God, the Almighty;
> Righteous and true are Your ways,
> King of the nations!
> Who will not fear, O Lord, and glorify Your name?
> For You alone are holy;

For ALL THE NATIONS WILL COME AND
WORSHIP BEFORE YOU,
FOR YOUR RIGHTEOUS ACTS HAVE BEEN
REVEALED." (Rev. 15:3-4).

John sees something like a sea of glass mixed with fire. It was not actually a sea of glass mixed with fire but that was the appearance it gave to John. Standing on the sea of glass were all those who had been victorious over the Beast. "After these things I looked, and behold, a great multitude which no one could count, from every nation and all tribes and peoples and tongues, standing before the throne and before the Lamb, clothed in white robes, and palm branches were in their hands"; (Rev. 7:9) "Then one of the elders answered, saying to me, "These who are clothed in the white robes, who are they, and where have they come from?" I said to him, "My lord, you know." And he said to me, "These are the ones who come out of the great tribulation," (Rev. 7:13-14). In Revelation Chapter 7 John tells us about a great multitude which no one could count standing before the throne praising God. These are the ones who come out of the great tribulation. These are the ones who had been victorious over the Beast and his image and the number of his name. These have not worshipped the Beast nor did they take the number of the Beast. These persevered through the times without succumbing to the temptation of Satan. Those victorious over the Beast have been washed in the blood of Jesus. The Word of God abides in them and they claim their victory through Christ Jesus. At the sound of the last trumpet, the end of the great tribulation, Jesus returns to earth and the dead in Christ rise first then those who are alive rise and meet Him in the air to be taken to heaven. In Chapter 7 and again here in Chapter 15 we find this great multitude before the throne praising God. These know that God alone is righteous and true in His ways. He is King of the nations. Which nations? He is King of all those nations who have knelt before Him and called Him King of kings and Lord of lords. Every nation and people and tongue that is left after the final battle will come and worship Him because His righteous acts have been revealed. From this day forward no one will ever turn their back on God. No one will ever again turn to worship another god. God alone is holy.

The song they sing is the song of Moses, the bond servant of God, and the Lamb. Moses represents the Law and Jesus is the fulfillment of the Law. The song says that the works of God are great and marvelous.

God is Almighty. God's ways are righteous and true. God is King of the nations. All will fear and glorify the name of God. Only God is holy. All will come and worship before God. And God's righteous acts have been revealed. The bottom line is the trial and tribulation and the wrath of God are all righteous acts of God. God is being praised because He has brought justice in destroying all evil. The song of Moses found in Exodus 15:1-21 praises God for His destruction of the Egyptians as they pursued Israel across the Red Sea. "Then Moses and the sons of Israel sang this song to the Lord, and said, "I will sing to the LORD, for He is highly exalted; the horse and its rider He has hurled into the sea." Ex. 15:1). The reader may wish to read the entire song of Moses found in Exodus chapter 15.

"After these things I looked, and the temple of the tabernacle of testimony in heaven was opened, and the seven angels who had the seven plagues came out of the temple, clothed in linen, clean and bright, and girded around their chests with golden sashes. Then one of the four living creatures gave to the seven angels seven golden bowls full of the wrath of God, who lives forever and ever. And the temple was filled with smoke from the glory of God and from His power; and no one was able to enter the temple until the seven plagues of the seven angels were finished" (Rev. 15:5-8). Seven angels come out of the temple of God and they are each given a bowl of wrath by one of the four living creatures. Then the temple was filled with smoke from the glory of God and no one was allowed to enter until the last bowl of wrath was poured out upon the earth. "Then the cloud covered the tent of meeting, and the glory of the LORD filled the tabernacle. Moses was not able to enter the tent of meeting because the cloud had settled on it, and the glory of the LORD filled the tabernacle." (Ex. 40:34-35). "It happened that when the priests came from the holy place, the cloud filled the house of the LORD, so that the priests could not stand to minister because of the cloud, for the glory of the LORD filled the house of the LORD." (1 Kings 8:10-11). Many times in the Old Testament Scriptures when the temple is filled with smoke no one could enter the temple. But when the smoke subsides, the temple is again opened. The smoke that fills the temple is the glory of God and the power of God. The presence is so strong that no one is able to stand being in its presence. The smoke will subside once the seven plagues have been poured out. The stage is now set for the wrath of God to begin.

CHAPTER 16

The Wrath of God

Read Chapter 16 of Revelation

"Then I heard a loud voice from the temple, saying to the seven angels, "Go and pour out on the earth the seven bowls of the wrath of God." (Rev. 16:1). The order to begin pouring out the bowls of wrath comes from the temple. When the angels came out of the temple and received the bowls from the living creature, the temple was filled with smoke of God's glory and power. When the temple is filled with God's glory and power no one is able to enter into the temple. The only one in the temple is God. Therefore, the order to begin pouring out the bowls of God's wrath comes from God Himself.

"So the first angel went and poured out his bowl on the earth; and it became a loathsome and malignant sore on the people who had the mark of the Beast and who worshipped his image." (Rev. 16:2). The first bowl of wrath brings forth malignant sores on those who have the mark of the Beast and worship him. This is everyone that is left on the earth. The saints have already gone to heaven to be with Jesus. The only ones left are those with the mark of the Beast.

"The second angel poured out his bowl into the sea, and it became blood like that of a dead man; and every living thing in the sea died." (Rev. 16:3). During the great tribulation, at the sound of the second trumpet, one third of the sea became blood and one third of the creatures die and one third of the ships were destroyed. Now the rest of the sea turns to blood and everything living in the sea dies. The sea becomes a rancid waste and all the food supply that the sea provided is gone.

"Then the third angel poured out his bowl into the rivers and the springs of waters; and they became blood. And I heard the angel of the waters saying, "Righteous are You, who are and who were, O Holy One, because You judged these things; for they poured out the blood of saints and prophets, and You have given them blood to drink. They deserve it." And I heard the altar saying, "Yes, O Lord God, the Almighty, true and righteous are Your judgments." (Rev. 16:4-7). Note that the angel refers to Jesus as the righteous One who is and was. He does not refer to Jesus as One who is to come. This further confirms that at this point Jesus has already come to gather His elect. Here, again with the sound of the third trumpet one third of the rivers and streams and springs became wormwood and bitter and unfit to drink. Now the rest of the fresh water supply become useless. There is now no fresh water to drink. At the opening of the fifth seal we saw the martyrs call out, "How long, O Lord will you refrain from judging and avenging our blood on those who dwell on earth?" The avenging began with the pouring out of the first bowl of wrath, but now, those who dwell on earth, who shed the blood of the martyrs, have to drink blood to survive.

"The fourth angel poured out his bowl upon the sun, and it was given to it to scorch men with fire. Men were scorched with fierce heat; and they blasphemed the name of God who has the power over these plagues, and they did not repent so as to give Him glory." (Rev. 16:8-9). At the sound of the fourth trumpet the days were shortened by one third. In spite of these short days the sun burns with such intensity that the people are actually scorched by its rays and its heat. Their answer to this is not to turn to God and repent. Rather, they curse God and blaspheme His name. There is no hope for those who remain. They refuse to repent so as to give God glory.

"Then the fifth angel poured out his bowl on the throne of the Beast, and his kingdom became darkened; and they gnawed their tongues because of pain, and they blasphemed the God of heaven because of their pains and their sores; and they did not repent of their deeds." (Rev. 16:10-11). The whole world becomes dark. There is no light whatsoever. The eyes are not capable of adjusting to the intense darkness and no one is able to see anything. The pain of the malignant sores and scorched skin is so severe that the people gnaw their tongues hoping to find some relief. And yet, in spite of their condition, they do not repent and turn to God for help.

"The sixth angel poured out his bowl on the great river, the Euphrates; and its water was dried up, so that the way would be prepared for the kings from the east." (Rev. 16:12). With the pouring out of the sixth bowl, the way is being prepared for the battle about to take place at Armageddon. "And I saw coming out of the mouth of the Dragon and out of the mouth of the Beast and out of the mouth of the False Prophet, three unclean spirits like frogs; for they are spirits of demons, performing signs, which go out to the kings of the whole world, to gather them together for the war of the great day of God, the Almighty. ("Behold, I am coming like a thief. Blessed is the one who stays awake and keeps his clothes, so that he will not walk about naked and men will not see his shame.") And they gathered them together to the place which in Hebrew is called Har-Magedon." (Rev. 16:13-16). The triune Satan; the Dragon, the Beast, and the False Prophet are sending forth demonic spirits to all the kings of the world to gather them together at Armageddon for battle. This is not a selective gathering of armies. This is all inclusive. The kings of the whole world will be so deceived that they will induct all their citizens into their armies in preparation for battle. Everyone remaining on earth will be summoned for the great day of God, the Almighty. Jesus says He is coming like a thief. No one will know the exact time of His arrival. Once they have been gathered together they should not relax. Jesus says they should remain clothed because when He comes there will be no time to get dressed and they will be caught shamefully naked. They will be caught with their pants down.

"Then the seventh angel poured out his bowl upon the air, and a loud voice came out of the temple from the throne, saying, "It is done." And there were flashes of lightning and sounds and peals of thunder; and there was a great earthquake, such as there had not been since man came to be upon the earth, so great an earthquake was it, and so mighty. The great city was split into three parts, and the cities of the nations fell. Babylon the great was remembered before God, to give her the cup of the wine of His fierce wrath. And every island fled away, and the mountains were not found. And huge hailstones, about one hundred pounds each, came down from heaven upon men; and men blasphemed God because of the plague of the hail, because its plague was extremely severe." (Rev. 16:17-21). It is done. That is, the wrath of God is complete. It ends with a grand finale. Flashes of lightening, loud sounds, peals of thunder, and earthquakes of extraordinary proportion will be experienced throughout the world. No one has ever seen anything like this before. And everyone throughout the whole world will see and experience the powerful wrath of God. The cities of the great nations will crumble to the ground. Babylon will be destroyed. Every island will disappear. The mountains will be flattened. The skies will open and pour forth one hundred pound hailstones upon all the people. And all the people will get angry with God and blaspheme His name. We just saw that Satan has gathered all the people of the world together for battle against God and His army. This grand display of God before the people excites their desires to conquer God and put Satan in charge. After all, a god who brings such destruction can be no god of theirs.

QUESTIONS CHAPTER 15 & 16

Read Revelation chapters 15 and 16

1. In a few Words what is it about?

Read Revelation 15:1

2. How many plagues are there?

3. What is the result of the plagues?

4. What does it mean, the wrath of God is complete?

Read Revelation15:2

5. Who are those who had been victorious over the Beast? See references below

Revelation 12:11

1 Corinthians 15:54-57

1 John 2:13, 14

1 John 4:3,4

1 John 5:5

Revelation 2:7, 11, 17

Read Revelation 15:3,4

    6. The song is identified with two people, who are they?

    7. What does Moses represent? See Leviticus 26:46; Joshua 1:7; 1 Kings 2:3; 2 Chronicles 30:16

    8. What does the Lamb represent? See Luke 24:44; John 1:17; John 1:45; Acts 13:38-40; Matthew 5:17

    9. What is the song of Moses and the Lamb about?

    10. What is the bottom line of the song?

    11. What is God praised for?

Read the Song of Moses Exodus 15:1-21

    12. What is this about?

    13. The seventh trumpet has blown. The saints have been taken to heaven. Wrath is about to come upon the world. The saints are standing on a sea of glass before the throne (Revelation 4:6) singing the song of Moses and the Lamb. Why?

Read Revelation 15:5, 6

    14. Where do the angels come from?

    15. Who's authority are they under?

Read Revelation 15:8

16. What was the temple filled with?

17. What was prohibited?

Read the following:

Exodus 40:34,35

1 Kings 8:10,11

2 Chronicles 5:13,14

18. How are these events similar to Revelation 15:8?

Read Revelation 16:1-7

19. What plagues have been brought upon the people?

20. What is the result of these plagues? See Revelation 16:6

21. How does this relate to Revelation 6:10?

Read Revelation 16:8-11

22. What plagues have been brought upon the people?

23. What was the result of these plagues? How did the people respond?

Read Revelation 16:12-16

24. What happens when the sixth angel pours out his bowl?

25. Has the battle of Har-Magedon occurred?

Read Revelation 16:17-21

26. List what happens when the seventh bowl is poured out.

CHAPTER 17

The Doom of Babylon

Read Chapter 17 of Revelation.

JOHN'S THIRD VISION

"**T**hen one of the seven angels who had the seven bowls came and spoke with me, saying, 'Come here, I will show you the judgment of the great harlot who sits on many waters, with whom the kings of the earth committed acts of immorality, and those who dwell on the earth were made drunk with the wine of her immorality. And he carried me away in the Spirit into a wilderness;'" (Rev. 17:1-3a). This begins John's third vision. We recognize the beginning of a vision when John writes, "He carried me away in the Spirit." Here John is carried away into a wilderness. The place where John is taken is not yet developed. It is, at John's time, a wilderness. The angel is going to show John the judgment of the great harlot who sits on many waters. A harlot is one who sells herself out in order to provide lustful pleasures for another. She not only provides lustful pleasure but she also tempts others to indulge in what she has to offer. The victims of this harlot are the kings of the earth. We will see in Chapter 18 that "those who dwell on earth" are people from all the nations of the earth and they are guilty of drinking the wine of her passion.

This third vision, presented in chapters 17 and 18 of Revelation, does not follow chronologically after John's second vision. Each vision stands by itself. We can determine when this vision occurs in reference to John's second vision because in Chapter 18 John hears a voice from heaven calling

God's people out of Babylon. Thus, this third vision must begin just prior to the blowing of the last trumpet when the church is removed from the earth and will end with the destruction of Babylon.

"and I saw a woman sitting on a scarlet Beast, full of blasphemous names, having seven heads and ten horns. The woman was clothed in purple and scarlet, and adorned with gold and precious stones and pearls, having in her hand a gold cup full of abominations and of the unclean things of her immorality, and on her forehead a name was written, a mystery, "BABYLON THE GREAT, THE MOTHER OF HARLOTS AND OF THE ABOMINATIONS OF THE EARTH." (Rev. 17:3b-5). The angel will explain the woman, and the Beast with seven heads and ten horns later in the chapter. But for now all we know is that the Beast was full of blasphemous names. Blasphemy is irreverence toward holy things, customs, or beliefs. Blasphemous means irreverent or profane. The Beast has only condemnation for God and for anyone who worships God. The woman is clothed like a harlot, covering her immorality with temptations of rich clothing and jewels. She offers abominations and unclean things of her immorality disguised in a golden cup as though these things should be greatly desired. On her forehead was written a mystery, "Babylon the great, the mother of harlots and of the abomination of the earth." As this woman is the mother of harlots and of abominations of the earth she is the source of all abominations and other harlots spring up from her. Under Nebuchadnezzar II, around 600 BC, Babylon became the most splendid city of the ancient world. Under Cyrus the Great, around 538 BC, Babylon became a center of learning and scientific advancement. And under the rule of Alexander, around 323 BC, Babylon again flourished as a center for learning and commerce. By 141 BC, Babylon was in complete desolation and would not rise again. However, for four hundred plus years Babylon was the center of commerce, culture, and scientific advancement. The Babylon of Revelation would be a great city or nation which is the center of commerce, culture, and scientific advancement for the world.

"And I saw the woman drunk with the blood of the saints, and with the blood of the witnesses of Jesus." (Rev. 17:6). "Therefore, behold, I am sending you prophets and wise men and scribes; some of them you will kill and crucify, and some of them you will scourge in your synagogues, and persecute from city to city, so that upon you may fall the guilt of all the righteous blood shed on earth, from the blood of righteous Abel to the blood of Zechariah, the son of Berechiah, whom you murdered between the temple and the altar. Truly I say to you, all these things will come upon this generation." (Matt. 23:34-36). Jesus says He was going to send prophets and wise men and scribes and the Scribes and Pharisees will kill them just as they killed others. And because they kill the prophets and scribes they are guilty of the blood of all the prophets and scribes killed or martyred for all times. The woman, Babylon, is drunk with the blood of the saints and witnesses because she was responsible for them being martyred. Their blood is on her hands.

"When I saw her, I wondered greatly. And the angel said to me, 'Why do you wonder? I will tell you the mystery of the woman and of the Beast that carries her, which has the seven heads and the ten horns. The Beast that you saw was, and is not, and is about to come up out of the Abyss and go to destruction. And those who dwell on the earth, whose name has not been written in the book of life from the foundation of the world, will wonder when they see the Beast, that he was and is not and will come.'" (Rev. 17:6-8). Jesus has been referred to as "Him who is and who was, and who is to come." (Rev. 1:4). The Beast is being described in the same way. The Beast will emulate the actions of Jesus in many ways, including being resurrected from the dead. This is the Antichrist. Those who dwell on earth, the unsaved, will wonder at his resurrection. But, the saints will not be fooled. After his resurrection he will then go on to destruction.

"Here is the mind which has wisdom. The seven heads are seven mountains on which the woman sits, and they are seven kings; five have fallen, one is, the other has not yet come; and when he comes, he must remain a little while. The Beast which was and is not, is himself also an eighth and is one of the seven, and he goes to destruction." (Rev. 17:9-11). The seven heads are now identified as seven nations or world powers. Five are in the past, one is, and one is yet to come. Going back in history we find the following world powers. At the time John wrote Revelation:

FIVE HAVE FALLEN

1st world power is Egypt in power around 1491 BC

2nd world power is Assyria in power around 1491-606 BC

3rd world power is Babylon in power around 606 - 538 BC

4th world power is Medo-Persia in power around 538-333 BC

5th world power is Greece in power around 333-44 BC

ONE IS

6th world power is Rome in power around 44 BC – 476 AD

ONE IS YET TO COME

There is no identity for the one yet to come. However it will be a great nation and will have major influence in world affairs. If the time of the end were today, 2011, we would say that the United States was this world power as it has more influence in the world than any other nation. Also, the United States was not in existence and the land was nothing but a wilderness at the time of John. Remember that John was in the wilderness when he saw this vision, which would indicate that the world power to come is a world power that springs up out of a wilderness. However, the end may not come for several hundred years yet and the United States may fall and some other power may rise to be a world power. In any case, we can look at the United States and see what type of a world power this may be. Whatever nation it may be, the ruler of the nation will be the Antichrist. At first he will not be known as the Antichrist but when he dies and is resurrected he will be an eighth ruler and he will set up his kingdom in Jerusalem and he will demand that he be worshipped.

"And he goes to destruction. The ten horns which you saw are ten kings who have not yet received a kingdom, but they receive authority as kings with the Beast for one hour. These have one purpose, and they give their power and authority to the Beast. These will wage war against the Lamb, and the Lamb will overcome them, because He is Lord of lords and King of kings, and those who are with Him are the called and chosen and faithful." (Rev. 17:11b-14). This is a preview of Chapter 19. We will see this in great detail there. Ten kings will rise up and join with the Beast. They will assemble all those on earth to wage war against Jesus and His saints. The battle will last but a short time, one hour. Jesus will overcome them, they will all be killed and the Beast will be destroyed.

"And he said to me, 'The waters which you saw where the harlot sits, are peoples and multitudes and nations and tongues. And the ten horns which you saw, and the Beast, these will hate the harlot and will make her desolate and naked, and will eat her flesh and will burn her up with fire. For God has put it in their hearts to execute His purpose by having a common purpose, and by giving their kingdom to the Beast, until the Words of God will be fulfilled. The woman whom you saw is the great city, which reigns over the kings of the earth.'" (Rev. 17:15-18). The harlot was earlier identified as Babylon. "Peoples, multitudes, nations and tongues" refers to the whole world. She is shown to have great influence over all the nations of the world. The seven heads of the Beast represent all the major world powers. The harlot has been influencing these world powers from the first to the last and her influence will not end until the battle at Armageddon. We do not know why the ten kings and the Beast hate the harlot. But it seems that God has caused them to hate the harlot so they will have a common enemy. Thus, they have a common purpose. The ten kings will unite together against the harlot under the leadership of the Beast. Once this begins it will last until the Words of God are fulfilled or until the end.

CHAPTER 18

Babylon is fallen

Read Chapter 18 of Revelation

"*A*fter these things I saw another angel coming down from heaven, having great authority, and the earth was illumined with his glory. And he cried out with a mighty voice, saying, 'Fallen, fallen is Babylon the great! She has become a dwelling place of demons and a prison of every unclean spirit, and a prison of every unclean and hateful bird. For all the nations have drunk of the wine of the passion of her immorality, and the kings of the earth have committed acts of immorality with her, and the merchants of the earth have become rich by the wealth of her sensuality.'" (Rev. 18:1-3). Babylon has fallen! "She has become," would indicate that she has not always been the way she is. She may in fact, at one time, have been a God fearing, God loving place. But not now. Now she has turned away from God. What happens when a nation turns its back on God? According to the prophet Jeremiah in Chapter 5, they do not see, they do not hear, they do not fear God, they have a stubborn and rebellious heart, they have turned aside and departed from God, they do not honor God who provides for them, wicked men dwell among God's people, they are fat and sleek, they excel in deeds of wickedness, they do not plead the cause of the orphan and they despise the poor, wicked men are found among my people, their houses are full of deceit and they catch men like a cage full of birds. Why has she become a dwelling place for demons and unclean spirits? Simply put, the demons and unclean spirits love her influence on the world. She is the source of the world's greed and selfish desires, nations are fed by her immorality and lusts, all the kings of the earth are immoral with her. She is a very rich nation and buys everything that she desires, everything that satisfies her quest for happiness and pleasure, and merchants have become rich by the wealth of her sensuality. Greed, lusts, and immorality are the things that attract Satan and his angels.

"I heard another voice from heaven, saying, 'Come out of her, my people, so that you will not participate in her sins and receive of her plagues; for her sins have piled up as high as heaven, and God has remembered her iniquities. Pay her back even as she has paid, and give back to her double according to her deeds; in the cup which she has mixed, mix twice as much for her. To the degree that she glorified herself and lived sensuously, to the same degree give her torment and mourning;' for she says in her heart, 'I SIT AS A QUEEN AND I AM NOT A WIDOW, and will never see mourning.' For this reason in one day her plagues will come, pestilence and mourning and famine, and she will be burned up with fire; for the Lord God who judges her is strong.'" (Rev. 18:4-8). Before God destroyed Sodom He sent His angels to Lot to warn His people so they would flee and not be caught in the destruction. "whomever you have in the city bring them out of the place, for we are about to destroy this place." (Gen. 19:12-13). Sodom was destroyed because it had become exceedingly wicked. Babylon has now become so wicked that there is no hope for return. Before God destroys the city He removes His people from its midst. The prophet Jeremiah in Chapter 50 spoke of an earlier destruction of Babylon which occurred in 500 BC. The reason for the destruction was: God's people were seeking God; their shepherds were leading them astray; they had forgotten who God is; their shepherds denied any guilt; so God says, "Get out of Babylon, I am about to destroy it"

And this Babylon would never rise again. "Therefore the desert creatures will live there along with the jackals; the ostriches also will live in it, and it will never again be inhabited or dwelt in from generation to generation." (Jer. 50:39). Therefore we cannot expect that the Babylon of Revelation is the old Babylon, rather it is a place like Babylon that has become a world leader in trade and finance. When Babylon speaks, the world listens. Babylon is a consuming nation and the world derives its wealth from its greed and insatiable lust. Babylon has become totally corrupt. Her sins have piled high as the heavens.

God is going to punish her, paying her back double according to her deeds, and tormenting her to the same degree that she glorified herself and lived sensually. Babylon has no good deeds. The only good deed is a deed that lifts up and glorifies God. Babylon lifts up and glorifies herself in all things. Babylon lives to satisfy her own sensual desires and conceit. Babylon sits as a queen and is not a widow and will never see mourning. Babylon believes she is invincible. Nothing and nobody can harm her. She needs no one. But God has another plan for her. "In one day her plagues will come, pestilence and mourning and famine, and she will be burned up with fire; for the Lord God who judges her is strong." As great and powerful as Babylon is it will only take a day for God to bring complete ruin to her.

"And the kings of the earth, who committed acts of immorality and lived sensuously with her, will weep and lament over her when they see the smoke of her burning, standing at a distance because of the fear of her torment, saying, 'Woe, woe, the great city, Babylon, the strong city! For in one hour your judgment has come.'" The ten kings will rise against Babylon to destroy her. It will be a swift and complete destruction. In just one hour Babylon will be in complete ruin.

"And the merchants of the earth weep and mourn over her, because no one buys their cargoes any more—cargoes of gold and silver and precious stones and pearls and fine linen and purple and silk and scarlet, and every kind of citron wood and every article of ivory and every article made from very costly wood and bronze and iron and marble, and cinnamon and spice and incense and perfume and frankincense and wine and olive oil and fine flour and wheat and cattle and sheep, and cargoes of horses and chariots and slaves and human lives. The fruit you long for has gone from you, and all things that were luxurious and splendid have passed away from you and men will no longer find them. The merchants of these things, who became rich from her, will stand at a distance because of the fear of her torment, weeping and mourning, saying, 'Woe, woe, the great city, she who was clothed in fine linen and purple and scarlet, and adorned with gold and precious stones and pearls; for in one hour such great wealth has been laid waste!' And every shipmaster and every passenger and sailor, and as many as make their living by the sea, stood at a distance, and were crying out as they saw the smoke of her burning, saying, 'What city is like the great city?' And they threw dust on their heads and were crying out, weeping and mourning, saying, 'Woe, woe, the great city, in which all who had ships at sea became rich by her wealth, for in one hour she has been laid waste!' Rejoice over her, O heaven, and you saints and apostles and prophets, because God has pronounced judgment for you against her." (Rev. 18:11-20). Babylon is further described as the main consumer of the world's goods. Every nation on earth depends on Babylon for their existence. It doesn't matter what goods you have, Babylon is your primary market. The merchants of the world have become rich in trading goods with Babylon and now stand in despair not knowing how they will survive. One moment Babylon is a hustling and bustling community and the next it is in ruin. There is no warning. In a blink of an eye it goes up in smoke. The news spreads quickly throughout the world as merchant ships full of cargo have no place to off load their goods. Everyone is amazed and shocked. It appears that the whole world is going to financial ruin. As you see what is happening to Babylon, consider this. Today, 2011, the United States of America is the consumer nation of the world. Practically every nation in the world depends on the U.S. to buy their goods and services. The United States not only imports goods but it also imports services. Much of its manufacturing is farmed out to foreign nations. Customer service and tech support is farmed out. The United States today has become a consumer nation rather than the producers of the world goods they once were. If the United States shut its borders and no longer bought foreign goods it would bring ruin and despair to the rest of the world. Now, let me make it clear that I do not in any way intend to say that the United States is the Babylon of the end times. However, what I do say is that the United States is in every way a type of the Babylon in the end times and we can fully understand the Babylon in Revelation by looking at what would happen if the United States fell to ruin today. The final message of this angel is "Rejoice over her O heavens and you saints and apostles and prophets because God has pronounced judgment for you against her." The great harlot, the one who entices the world to drink the wine of her passion, has been destroyed. The one who made it difficult for Christians to live in peace and comfort has been destroyed. The one who has killed the prophets and apostles is destroyed. All praise to God Almighty because His justice has prevailed.

"Then a strong angel took up a stone like a great millstone and threw it into the sea, saying, 'So will Babylon, the great city, be thrown down with violence, and will not be found any longer. And the sound of harpists and musicians and flute-players and trumpeters will not be heard in you any longer; and no craftsman of any craft will be found in you any longer; and the sound of a mill will not be heard in you any longer, and the light of a lamp will not shine in you any longer; and the voice of the bridegroom and bride will not be heard in you any longer; for your merchants were the great men of the earth, because all the nations were deceived by your sorcery. And in her was found the blood of prophets and of saints and of all who have been slain on the earth.'" (Rev. 18:21-24). Here is the full extent of the destruction of Babylon. Nothing is left. There is no rejoicing and singing and playing of music in Babylon. No crafts will be made in Babylon. No mills will be running. There will be no recovery for this great city. But worse than any of this is that the church has been removed and is no longer there. The Light of the Lamp, the gospel message, has ceased to be preached. There is nothing good left in Babylon.

There are a few clues that help us to put a time frame on the destruction of Babylon. Our best clue comes at the end of this passage. "The voice of the bridegroom and bride will not be heard in you any longer." The church and the Holy Spirit have been removed. This will happen at the sound of the last trumpet. And in verse 4 the angel say, "Come out of her my people." God is about ready to destroy Babylon but He first removes His people. The wrath of God begins with the destruction of Babylon. How long will it take? It will take only one hour. Ten nations will be gathered together. They will come up against Babylon and will totally destroy the entire place.

We do not know what drives these ten nations to come up against Babylon. It may be that the Antichrist has now risen to power. He has established himself as God desiring all to worship him. However, although the people do worship him, they still look in favor towards Babylon as it is their source of wealth. This makes the Antichrist jealous and he hates Babylon so he gathers ten nations together with the express purpose of annihilating Babylon. The mission takes but one hour. This is a bit of speculation and is not intended to be derived from Scripture. It is only provided as a possibility as to how this may happen. What we know is, God has caused them to hate Babylon and He has caused the Beast to hate Babylon and they have joined forces to see to it that Babylon is totally destroyed.

Keeping in mind our sequence of events:

/opening of seven seals/blowing of seven trumpets/saints removed/

1260 days	1260 days
Antichrist arrives	Antichrist revealed
	Beast exercises authority
	Destruction of Babylon

pouring out of seven bowls of wrath/
30 days

(See full time line in the appendix)

QUESTIONS CHAPTER 17 & 18

BABYLON

Read Revelation Chapters 17, 18

Revelation17:3

1. Where was John when he had this vision?

THE BEAST

Read Revelation 17:7-13

2. What is this a picture of? See Revelation 17:8

3. Compare to Revelation 13:3,4 Is it the same?

Read Revelation 17:9,10

4. What does this say the seven heads are?

5. Turn to the last page of your homework and see what six world powers have dominated the world in history. What are those six world powers?

6. What empire was in power at the time John wrote Revelation?

7. What do you think the seventh head represents?

Read Revelation 17:11

8. What does it say about the Beast?

Read Revelation 17:12, 13

9. When will the ten horns receive their power?

10. How long will they be in power?

11. What is their purpose?

Read Revelation 17:14

12. What will the Beast and ten kings do?

13. Who will be with the Lamb?

Read Revelation 17:16-18

14. What is the relationship between the Beast and ten kings and Babylon?

15. Why will Babylon be destroyed?

16. What is the relationship of Babylon to the rest of the world?

17. From the following how would you describe this Babylon?

    Revelation 17:2

    Revelation 17:4

    Revelation 17:5

Revelation 17:6

Revelation 17:15

Revelation 17:18

Revelation 18:2

Revelation 18:3

Revelation 18:11-14

Revelation 18:15

Revelation 18:24

The history books show us that there have been world empires in the past. This began with Egypt and the time of the pharaohs, which is also the time period that the children of Israel were in bondage and from which they were delivered.

The next world empire to come on the scene was Assyria, and it was this world empire that was in place during the time of the prophet Jeremiah

After Assyria the next world empire, Babylon appears on the world stage. It's king Nebuchadnezzar's experiences with the prophet Daniel is well documented in the book of Daniel in the Bible.

The following world empire, still with the prophet Daniel in the picture, was Medo/Persia, a coalition government.

It in turn was succeeded by the world empire that was Greece under Alexander the Great. Alexander's empire was all encompassing even if short-lived.

The next, and to-date last, world empire to see the light was that of the Roman Empire under which Christ was born and the disciples lived and worked preaching the Gospel and teaching all the world of the truth in Christ.

Never since the disintegration of the Roman Empire, first into East Rome and West Rome, and then just generally falling apart without ever having been conquered or vanquished, has there been a complete world empire

The Chronology of World History

1st world power = EGYPT (in power to 1491 BC)

2nd world power=ASSYRIA (1491 - 606 BC)

3rd world power=BABYLON (606 - 538 BC)

4th world power=Medo/Persia (538 - 333 BC)

5th world power=GREECE (333 - 44 BC)

6th world power=ROME (44 BC - 476 AD)

CHAPTER 19

Preparing for the Millennium

Read Chapter 19 of Revelation

*F*our things are happening in Chapter 19: Babylon has fallen and God is praised for His justice; the marriage of the Lamb; the battle at Armageddon; and the doom of the Beast and the False Prophet. These things are all being done in preparation for the thousand year reign of Christ on the present earth. These four things seem to be the main things that must be accomplished before God sets up His reign on earth.

"After these things I heard something like a loud voice of a great multitude in heaven, saying, "Hallelujah! Salvation and glory and power belong to our God; BECAUSE HIS JUDGMENTS ARE TRUE AND RIGHTEOUS; for He has judged the great harlot who was corrupting the earth with her immorality, and HE HAS AVENGED THE BLOOD OF HIS BOND-SERVANTS ON HER." And a second time they said, "Hallelujah! HER SMOKE RISES UP FOREVER AND EVER." And the twenty-four elders and the four living creatures fell down and worshiped God who sits on the throne saying, "Amen. Hallelujah!" And a voice came from the throne, saying, "Give praise to our God, all you His bond-servants, you who fear Him, the small and the great." Then I heard something like the voice of a great multitude and like the sound of many waters and like the sound of mighty peals of thunder, saying, "Hallelujah! For the Lord our God, the Almighty, reigns." (Rev. 19:1-6).

Who do we find praising God?

First there is a great multitude, that is "those who come out of the great tribulation and they have washed their robes and made them white in the blood of Jesus," (Rev. 7:14);

second, there are "all, you, His bondservants" that is all those of all times who have accepted Christ as their Lord and Savior and serve Him;

third, there are the twenty-four elders and four living creatures;

and finally there is a voice from the throne, this is not specifically identified but is likely the angels.

Based on this we can say that this event happens after all the saints are taken to heaven at the sound of the last trumpet.

Why are they rejoicing and praising God? There are five reasons:

First, because "Salvation, glory, and power belong to our God." God has gathered together His elect and has established that He is the One who brings salvation, that He alone is to be glorified, and that He has power over all things in heaven and on earth.

Second, because "His judgments are righteous and true." He has told us in His Law what He expects of us. His Law is impossible for mankind to obey perfectly all of the time. And those who do not obey the Law are condemned. But God has given us One who is perfect to fulfill every requirement of the Law. Those who accept His grace are redeemed and judged "not guilty." What man could not do, God has done. His judgments are true and they are righteous altogether.

Third, He has judged the great harlot who was corrupting the earth. He has destroyed Babylon.

Fourth, He has avenged the blood of His bond servants. Those bond servants who have been killed by Babylon because of their faith have been avenged by its destruction.

The fifth thing they are praising God and rejoicing over is that finally the Lord our God, the Almighty reigns. God has taken all power and authority away from Satan and is about to bring him and his followers to destruction.

"Let us rejoice and be glad and give the glory to Him, for the marriage of the Lamb has come and His bride has made herself ready." It was given to her to clothe herself in fine linen, bright and clean; for the fine linen is the righteous acts of the saints. Then he said to me, "Write, 'Blessed are those who are invited to the marriage supper of the Lamb.'" He said to me, "These are true words of God." Then I fell at his feet to worship him. But he said to me, "Do not do that; I am a fellow servant of yours and your brethren who hold the testimony of Jesus; worship God. For the testimony of Jesus is the spirit of prophecy." (Rev. 19:7-10). The bride is the church. The marriage of the church and Jesus has come. The courtship is over. There is no more gospel to preach. There are no more altar calls. The church is now complete. All those who would prepare themselves for the wedding have now done so. They have all "clothed themselves in fine linen, bright and clean, which is the righteous acts of the saints." The righteous acts of the saints are those things which lift up and glorify God. Anything that does not lift up and glorify God is unrighteous. The saints have had their clothes washed in the blood of Jesus. All those things that disgrace God have been washed out. The only acts left are those which glorify God. These are the fine white linen clothes of the saints.

Who is invited to the marriage supper? "go into all the world and preach the gospel to all creation." (Mark 16:15). Everyone is invited but not everyone will accept the invitation. Who will accept the invitation? "whosoever believeth in Jesus shall not die, but have life eternal" (John 3:16), "Whoever will call on the name of the Lord will be saved." (Rom. 10:13), "whoever loses his life for My sake will save it." (Luke 9:24), "whoever confesses that Jesus is the Son of God, God abides in him, and he in God." (1 John 4:15). Everyone who believes in Jesus, everyone who calls on the name of Jesus, everyone who gives up his life for Jesus, and everyone who confesses that Jesus is God have accepted the invitation and are at the marriage supper of the Lamb. Jesus has promised that we will see this day. "In my Father's house are many dwelling places . . . . for I go to prepare a place for you and I will come again and receive you to myself." (John 14:2-3). Those who believe in Christ Jesus as their Lord and Savior can rest assured that they are included in the marriage supper of the Lamb and will be with Him forever and ever.

John falls at the feet of the angel who brings him the message and the angel tells him not to do that. Worship God. God and only God is to be worshipped.

"And I saw heaven opened, and behold, a white horse, and He who sat on it is called Faithful and True, and in righteousness He judges and wages war. His eyes are a flame of fire, and on His head are many diadems; and He has a name written on Him which no one knows except Himself. He is clothed with a robe dipped in blood, and His name is called The Word of God. And the armies which are in heaven, clothed in fine linen, white and clean, were following Him on white horses. From His mouth comes a sharp sword, so that with it He may strike down the nations, and He will rule them with a rod of iron; and He treads the wine press of the fierce wrath of God, the Almighty. And on His robe and on His thigh He has a name written, "KING OF KINGS, AND LORD OF LORDS." (Rev. 19:11-16). Jesus rides in on a white horse followed by the saints. He has a mission. He judges and wages war. He is not coming in peace. His eyes are a flame of fire. He has many crowns on His head. He is King of kings and Lord of lords. From his mouth comes a sharp sword and with it He strikes down the nations. All the nations, all those who are left on the earth, are condemned and put to death by the Word of God. He treads the wine press of the fierce wrath of God. The wrath of God is about to be completed.

"Then I saw an angel standing in the sun, and he cried out with a loud voice, saying to all the birds which fly in mid-heaven, "Come, assemble for the great supper of God, so that you may eat the flesh of kings and the flesh of commanders and the flesh of mighty men and the flesh of horses and of those who sit on them and the flesh of all men, both free men and slaves, and small and great." And I saw the Beast and the kings of the earth and their armies assembled to make war against Him who sat on the horse and against His army." (Rev. 19:17-19). Preparations are being made for the battle. Even the vultures are being prepared to clean up the mess that will be left. John saw the Beast and the kings of the earth and their armies on one side and Jesus and His army on the other. In Chapter 16 we read about the preparation for this. The Dragon, the Beast and the False Prophet send forth evil spirits to deceive the nations and to gather them all together for the war of the great day of God. The place they gathered was Har-Magedon, or Armageddon. And now, the battle is about to take place. Everything has been prepared and both armies are assembled and poised to go to battle.

"And the Beast was seized, and with him the False Prophet who performed the signs in his presence, by which he deceived those who had received the mark of the Beast and those who worshiped his image; these two were thrown alive into the lake of fire which burns with brimstone. And the rest were killed with the sword which came from the mouth of Him who sat on the horse, and all the birds were filled with their flesh." (Rev. 19:20-21). Of course, they did not stand a chance. First their leaders were seized, the Beast, or Antichrist, and the False Prophet. These were thrown into the lake of fire and would never be heard from again. And then the rest were killed. In other words, no one was left on earth. All have been killed and the earth has been purged of the influence of the Beast and the False Prophet. They will no longer deceive anyone. They have been terminated. And all those who have followed the Beast will no longer deceive and sway others to follow the Beast. There is no danger from the Beast and the False Prophet. They have been thrown into the lake of fire and there is no remaining influence of the followers of the Beast. The mess has now been cleaned up by the birds in mid-heaven. There is but one thing left to do before God can set up His kingdom on earth. Satan remains to be dealt with.

Questions Chapter 19

Read Revelation Chapter 19

Read Revelation 19:1-6

1. Who is praising God and rejoicing?

2. What five things are they rejoicing over?

3. What is the bottom line?

Read Revelation 19:7-10

4. What does Revelation19:7 mean?

5. Who is the bride?

6. In what way has the bride made herself ready?

7. What is the fine linen? What are righteous acts?

8. Why are the linen clothes not soiled?

9. Who is invited to the marriage supper of the Lamb? See John 3:16; Romans 10:13 John 12:46; Mark 16:16

10. Who accepts the invitation? See John 3:36; John 6:40; John 11:25 Luke 9:24; 1John 4:15

11. What is the testimony of Jesus? See John 14:2-3; John 14:6; John 14:10-11; John 14:16-18; John 14:26;

Read Revelation 19:11-19

12. What is this about?

13. When does it happen on your timeline?

14. Who is leading on the white horse?

15. Who is following Him?

16. Who is assembled to fight against Jesus and His army?

Read Revelation 19:20-21

17. What happens to the Beast and the False Prophet?

18. Who is the Beast?

19. What happens to the rest?

20. Who is left to inhabit the earth?

CHAPTER 20

The Millennium

Read Chapter 20 of Revelation

" hen I saw an angel coming down from heaven, holding the key of the Abyss and a great chain in his hand. And he laid hold of the Dragon, the serpent of old, who is the Devil and Satan, and bound him for a thousand years; and he threw him into the Abyss, and shut it and sealed it over him, so that he would not deceive the nations any longer, until the thousand years were completed; after these things he must be released for a short time." (Rev. 20:1-3). The Dragon, Satan, is now being dealt with. But this is only temporary. He is bound for a thousand years and thrown into the Abyss and the Abyss is sealed shut. There is no way for the Dragon to get out. He cannot have any influence over the world. His removal from the world is total and complete. But, God is not through with him yet. When the thousand years are over he will be released to do his final job.

"Then I saw thrones, and they sat on them, and judgment was given to them. And I saw the souls of those who had been beheaded because of their testimony of Jesus and because of the Word of God, and those who had not worshiped the Beast or his image, and had not received the mark on their forehead and on their hand; and they came to life and reigned with Christ for a thousand years. The rest of the dead did not come to life until the thousand years were completed. This is the first resurrection. Blessed and holy is the one who has a part in the first resurrection; over these the second death has no power, but they will be priests of God and of Christ and will reign with Him for a thousand years." (Rev. 20:4- 6).

Who is described here? There are thrones and those who sat on them, the twenty-four elders; there are the souls of those who were martyred; and there are those who had not worshipped the Beast or his image and had not received the mark of the Beast. All those who are destined for eternal life are before the throne. And they came to life to reign with Christ for a thousand years. This is the first resurrection. The second resurrection will be the resurrection of the lost souls after the thousand years are completed. Note that at the sound of the last trumpet the dead in Christ rose to meet Him in the air and those who were alive were transformed and joined them. All of the saints at that point were bodily taken to heaven but their bodies were transformed into heavenly beings. Now all of these are resurrected with physical bodies capable of living on earth. "Blessed and holy is the one who has a part in the first resurrection; over these the second death has no power." The saints are born to live on this earth, they die, and they are resurrected to eternal life never to die again. That is, they live twice and die once. The unsaved are born to live on this earth, they die, they will be resurrected again, the second resurrection, and they will die again. They live twice and they die twice.

At this point Christ is reigning on the present earth. The saints, those who had died in Christ and those who were taken up to heaven at the rapture, are being resurrected to reign with Him. The rest of the dead remain dead but they will be resurrected when the thousand years are completed. The Beast and the False Prophet are thrown into the lake of fire never to be heard from again. And Satan is bound up in the Abyss waiting for his release.

"When the thousand years are completed, Satan will be released from his prison, and will come out to deceive the nations which are in the four corners of the earth, Gog and Magog, to gather them together for the war; the number of them is like the sand of the seashore. And they came up on the broad plain of the earth and surrounded the camp of the saints and the beloved city, and fire came down from heaven and devoured them. And the Devil who deceived them was thrown into the lake of fire and brimstone, where the Beast and the False Prophet are also; and they will be tormented day and night forever and ever." (Rev. 20:7-10). The thousand years are completed and Satan is released. He comes out and deceives the nations. Who are the nations? Remember, "The rest of the dead did not come to life until the thousand years were completed." They have now come alive. The nations are the rest of the dead who have been resurrected at the second resurrection. They are in the four corners of the earth. That is, they are in the north, south, east and west. They are all there is on the earth except the saints which are in the holy city. Everyone who died without knowing Christ will be in their numbers. Satan deceives them. He convinces them that they have not been beaten. After all they were dead and now they are alive. They are invincible. He will lead them to victory and they can take over the world once and for all. He gathers them all together. Their numbers are as the sand of the seashore. Who could possibly defeat such an army? They come up to the holy city where the saints are gathered with the idea that they will simply charge the city, kill everyone and then they will own the world and never be bothered by these religious fanatics again. Obviously they don't know God. When they come upon the city, God rains fire down on them and devours them. Satan, the Devil who deceived them, is thrown into the lake of fire where the Beast and the False Prophet are. They will be tormented forever and ever but they will never be heard from again.

"Then I saw a great white throne and Him who sat upon it, from whose presence earth and heaven fled away, and no place was found for them. And I saw the dead, the great and the small, standing before the throne, and books were opened; and another book was opened, which is the book of life; and the dead were judged from the things which were written in the books, according to their deeds. And the sea gave up the dead which were in it, and death and Hades gave up the dead which were in them; and they were judged, every one of them according to their deeds. Then death and Hades were thrown into the lake of fire. This is the second death, the lake of fire. And if anyone's name was not found written in the book of life, he was thrown into the lake of fire." (Rev. 20:11-15). This is the great white throne judgment. This is the final judgment. All of the dead, the great and the small are standing before the throne. Those who are alive, the saints, are not a part of this. They have accepted the blood of Christ Jesus as payment for their sin and have been declared not guilty. The righteousness of Christ has been imputed to them and they stand righteous before God. But all the rest come before the throne. And the books are opened and another book is opened. The books containing all the deeds of the dead are spread open and the dead are all judged according to their deeds. No one will escape this judgment. God is a just God and will not pronounce punishment until guilt has been established. Each will be repaid according to his or her deeds. The other book is the book of life. The saints would find their name written in this book. They do not have to worry about this judgment. Just to be sure, the book is checked for each one before the throne to see if his or her name is there. Anyone whose name is not there is thrown into the lake of fire. There is no resurrection from the lake of fire. This is final. It is over for them. Likewise, death and Hades are also thrown into the lake of fire. There will be no more death. There will be no more Hades. Hades is no longer necessary, as it was for the souls of the lost. Hades is empty and no one will ever go there again. Therefore, Hades is destroyed in the lake of fire.

QUESTIONS CHAPTER 20

Read Revelation Chapter 20

    1.   List the main points of Revelation 20

Read Revelation 20:1-3

    2.   Read Revelation 1:18 Who has the keys of death and Hades?

    3.   Read Revelation 9:1 Who now has the key of the bottomless pit?

    4.   Is Hades, the bottomless and the Abyss all the same?

    5.   How does one gain access to the Abyss?

    6.   Lest we be confused John wants us to know who is being bound up. How does he describe him?

Read Revelation 12:9

    7.   What does it say about Satan?

    8.   Why was Satan thrown into and locked in the Abyss?

    9.   At this point in time who inhabits the earth?

        What happened at the seventh trumpet?

        What happened in Revelation 19:20?

What happened in Revelation 19:21?

What happened in Revelation 20:3?

What will happen at the end of 1000 years?

Read Revelation 20:4-6

10. Who comes to life to reign with Christ?

11. What happens to the rest of the dead?

12. What is this called?

13. What does Revelation 20:6 say about those who take part in the first resurrection?

Read Revelation 2:11

14. What does this say?

Read Revelation 20:14

15. What does this say?

16. What happens to those who take part in the first resurrection?

Read Revelation 1:6

17. What has Christ made us to be?

Read Revelation 5:10

18. How does Rev 20:14 relate to this?

Read Revelation 20:7-10

19. What happens in Revelation 20:7?

20. Who does Satan deceive?

21. Where did they come from? See Revelation 20:5

22. How does this relate to:

Ezekiel 7:2

Ezekiel 38:2

Ezekiel 39:1, 6

23. How many people will come to life to join Satan?

Read Revelation 20:9

24. Where are the saints gathered?

Read Ezekiel 38:9, 16

25. How does this relate?

26. How is Satan defeated?

Read Ezekiel 38:22

    27. Is this the same?

    28. What happens to Satan's army?

Read Revelation20:10

    29. What happens to Satan?

Read Revelation20:11-15

    30. Where does this scene take place?

Read Revelation20:12-13

    31. Who is being judged?

    32. What do the following say?

        Matthew 16:27

        Psalm 62:12

        Proverb 24:12

        Romans 2:6-8

        Romans 14:!2

        1st Corinthians 3:13-14

        Revelation 2:23

Read Revelation 20:14-15

    33. What is done away with in Revelation 20:14?

Read 1ˢᵗ Corinthians 15:26

    34. What does this say?

    35. Why do you think death and Hades are destroyed?

    36. What is the second death?

    37. Who partakes in the second death?

    38. What does Revelation 20:6 say regarding the saints?

At the conclusion of Chapter 20

    39. Who is left?

    40. What or who has been destroyed?

CHAPTER 21

New Heaven and New Earth

Read Chapter 21 of Revelation

*W*e still have the current heavens and the current earth. The final kingdom is about to be established. But we still have a problem. The current heavens and the current earth are still under the curse of God brought on by the first sin. The Scriptures here that refer to the heavens are referring to the atmosphere above the earth's surface. Prior to the flood the earth's atmosphere was closed and the earth enjoyed the benefit of a very controlled environment. There was no rain upon the earth and there were no storms. But when God brought the floods upon the earth He opened the atmosphere and now there are violent storms with lightening, thunder, violent winds that destroy everything in their path and flooding rains. The saints are living on the earth. Jesus is with the saints on the earth. Living in this world will not be all pleasurable. There will still be storms, floods, earth quakes, hot burning summers and cold freezing winters. There will still be weeds to infest the gardens and insects that bite and destroy crops. There will still be wild animals. However the body has been purified and glorified. There will be no more sickness, pain, suffering or death. But the things that were brought upon the earth and heavens by the curse still remain.

JOHN'S FOURTH VISION

"Then I saw a New Heaven and a New Earth; for the first heaven and the first earth passed away, and there is no longer any sea." (Rev. 21:1-1). Now a New Heaven and New Earth appear. The old heaven and old earth have passed away. The prophet Isaiah writes, "For behold I create New Heavens and a New Earth, and the former things will not be remembered or come to mind." (Isa. 65:17). Not only will there be a New Heaven and New Earth but we will no longer remember the old, they will not even come to mind. We will have no recollection of storms. We will have no recollection of earthquakes. There will be no weeds in our gardens and we will not remember the many hours we spent on our knees pulling weeds and trying to get all the roots out. There will be no more mosquitoes or gnats or any other biting and stinging insects and again we will not have any knowledge that they ever existed. We will not need bug spray, or insecticides, or weed killer, or heavy warm clothes, or air conditioning, or hurricane protection, or fences to protect our property from thieves, or courts to settle arguments with those who try to harm us, or movie ratings to protect us from unfit movies, or dress codes, and we can go on and on. The current world is full of corruption and things that make our life miserable and require us to put up defense mechanisms to protect us from evil. There is no escaping the effects of this sinful world. We cannot even imagine what it would be like to live in a world where everything is pure and wholesome, where we no longer need any protection from the evils of this world. But that is what the New Heaven and New Earth will be like. To remember the way things were would make us sad to think that the world could ever be that way. So God will erase any memory of it from our minds. "the New Heavens and the New Earth which I will make will endure before Me." (Isa. 66:22) The New Heaven and the New Earth are eternal. They will not decay and they will never be cursed. We live in a world today that is in a state of decay. Every day things digress to a worse and worse condition. And things will continue to get worse and worse until this heaven and earth are destroyed. But the New Heaven and New Earth will not decay. They are eternally perfect, and pure and holy.

Not only do we have the corrupt physical world to deal with today but we have people who are evil and corrupt. We have to be constantly on our guard against those who would hurt us physically, emotionally and spiritually. We have fences and door locks and security systems and courts and guns, and private schools, and movie ratings, and private clubs, and all sorts of ways and devices to protect us from others who tempt us to go the way of Satan, to get angry, upset, talk ugly, and work to get even and have our blood avenged. "But according to His promise, we are looking for New Heavens and a New Earth, in which righteousness dwells." (2 Peter 3:13) Yes! Everything and everybody is righteous and good! No more stress, no more anxiety, no more anger, no more upsetting situations. We will live in peace with all people. And we will not remember the old way of life at all.

What happened to the old heaven and old earth? "The present heavens and earth are being reserved for fire, kept for the day of judgment and destruction of ungodly men. But the day of the Lord will come like a thief, in which the heavens will pass away with a roar and the elements will be destroyed with intense heat, and the earth and its works will be burned up." (Peter 3:7, 10). The old heaven and old earth will be used as a place of destruction. Once the saints have been removed, God will begin the process of first purging the earth of all evil people and evil beings. Then, after His thousand year reign on earth, He will sweep away the heavens with a roar and disintegrate the heavens and the earth with intense heat so that nothing is left. And the saints will inhabit the New Earth whose climate is under the influence of the New Heavens.

And I saw the holy city, New Jerusalem, coming down out of heaven from God, made ready as a bride adorned for her husband. And I heard a loud voice from the throne, saying, "Behold, the tabernacle of God is among men, and He will dwell among them, and they shall be His people, and God Himself will be among them" (Rev. 21:2-3). God is able to bring His tabernacle down to earth. Now that the New Heaven and New Earth have been created God will live on the New Earth with us. We will never be separated from God. He will dwell among us, He will be our God, and we will be His people. The New Jerusalem is the city that Abraham was hoping for. "By faith Abraham, when he was called obeyed by going out to a place which he was to receive for an inheritance . . . . By faith he lived as an alien in the land of promise . . . . for he was looking for the city which has foundations, and whose architect and builder is God . . . . He did not receive the promises, but he welcomed them from a distance, having confessed that they were strangers and exiles on the earth. For those who say such things make it clear that they are seeking a country of their own . . . . They desire a better country, that is, a heavenly one. Therefore God is not ashamed to be called their God; for He has prepared a city for them." (Heb. 11 parts of 13-16). Abraham foresaw the city of Jerusalem which is in heaven and he longed to reside there. Abraham was looking for the New Jerusalem. The promise, though seen and welcomed, has not been realized. All the past and present saints long for and seek a better place in heaven. And God has prepared a city for them. The city is now in heaven and those who die in Christ will see and inhabit the New Jerusalem as they await the creation of the New Heaven and New Earth. They will see the New Jerusalem come down out of the sky and land on the New Earth. What a glorious day that will be. The city will be "made ready as a bride adorned for her husband." That means it will be gorgeous! Everything about the city will be perfect and pure and holy. "Behold the tabernacle of God is among men and He will dwell among them." Can you imagine that? We will be in the very presence of God. I mean, we will be in the very physical presence of God, not the spiritual presence as we are today. We will see Him on His throne and Jesus will walk the streets among us. We will be face to face with God and His Son Jesus every single day. This is the fulfillment of one of God's oldest and greatest promises. "Moreover I will make My dwelling among you." (Lev. 26:11). "I will set My sanctuary in their midst forever. My dwelling place also will be with them; and I will be their God, and they will be My people." (Ezek. 37:26-27).

"and He will wipe away every tear from their eyes; and there will no longer be any death; there will no longer be any mourning, or crying, or pain; the first things have passed away." (Rev. 21:4). All the things that cause sadness, discomfort and pain will have passed away. There will be no more misery, no more pain, no more death, and no more suffering. God will wipe away the tears before they even form. "He will swallow up death for all time, and the Lord God will wipe tears away from all faces, and he will wipe the reproach of His people from all the earth." (Isa. 25:8) "And the ransomed of the LORD will return and come with joyful shouting to Zion, with an everlasting joy upon their heads. They will find gladness and joy, and sorrow and sighing will flee away." (Isa. 35:10). Yes, even disappointment will flee away. Not even a hint of thinking that things could be better. This is not simply as good as it gets, this is as good as it could ever possibly be.

"And He who sits on the throne said, "Behold, I am making all things new." And He said, "Write, for these Words are faithful and true." Then He said to me, "It is done. I am the Alpha and the Omega, the beginning and the end. I will give to the one who thirsts from the spring of the water of life without cost. He who overcomes will inherit these things, and I will be his God and he will be My son. But for the cowardly and unbelieving and abominable and murderers and immoral persons and sorcerers and idolaters and all liars, their part will be in the lake that burns with fire and brimstone, which is the second death." (Rev. 21:5-8). God says He is making all things new. We read in verse one that the old heaven and old earth had passed away. That is, they were no more. Everything on the old earth and in the old heavens was corrupt and would not be fit for the New Heaven and New Earth. Because of sin God brought a curse upon all of creation. In the New Heaven and New Earth there will be no curse. Nothing of the old is fit for the new. Therefore God recreates everything perfect and holy and undefiled. He says these Words are faithful and true. God does not lie. God cannot lie. We can believe what He says down to the very letter. It is done. There is nothing else to do. God is eternal, has always been and will always be, He has the first and last Word in all things. Nothing is done, said, or thought except by and through Him. He was from the very beginning. "In the beginning was the Word, and the Word was with God, and the Word was God. He was in the beginning with God. All things came into being through Him, and apart from Him nothing came into being." (John 1:1-3). God has been since a time before the very beginning of creation. Everything that has been or will be created was created by God through Christ Jesus. He will give to the one who thirsts from the spring of the water of life without cost. When did this water become available? Was it only available after the coming of Jesus? No. "Ho! Every one who thirsts, come to the waters; And you who have no money come, buy and eat. Come, buy wine and milk without money and without cost . . . . Listen carefully to Me, and eat what is good, and delight yourself in abundance. Incline your ear and come to Me. Listen, that you may live;" (Isa. 55:1-3). God's living water has been available since the beginning of time. The water is free. There is no cost. All those who believe and trust in God may drink of the living water and have life eternal. Those who overcome, that is, those who do not fall into sin by following Satan, will inherit these things. God will be their Father and they will be His son. A father is one who loves, cares for, attends to the needs of his children. He protects his children through every circumstance of life. What better Father could we have? No one has a greater love than God. God loved the world so much that He gave His only Son so that we may have life eternal. No one is more capable of providing for his children than God. He knows our needs before we do. And He wraps His loving arms around us so that no harm could ever come to us. To be a son of God means that He brought us into this world and will care for our every need. He loves us and will protect us in all things. His loving kindness will never ever depart from us. But those who take the mark of the Beast and follow him, they will have their place in the lake of fire. This is the second death from which there is no return. "He who overcomes will not be hurt by the second death." (Rev. 2:11).

John's Fourth Vision

"Then one of the seven angels who had the seven bowls full of the seven last plagues came and spoke with me, saying, "Come here, I will show you the bride, the wife of the Lamb. And he carried me away in the Spirit to a great and high mountain, and showed me the holy city, Jerusalem, coming down out of heaven from God, having the glory of God. Her brilliance was like a very costly stone, as a stone of crystal-clear jasper. It had a great and high wall, with twelve gates, and at the gates twelve angels; and names were written on them, which are the names of the twelve tribes of the sons of Israel. There were three gates on the east and three gates on the north and three gates on the south and three gates on the west. And the wall of the city had twelve foundation stones, and on them were the twelve names of the twelve apostles of the Lamb." (Rev. 21:9-14). This is the fourth and last vision. John was carried away in the spirit. He was carried to a great high mountain where he saw the New Jerusalem coming down out of heaven. The city is described in all its glory. It had the brilliance like that of crystal clear jasper. We can imagine that the city had the brilliance of a very large, fine colorless diamond. It had a high wall with twelve gates. On each gate was the name of one of the twelve tribes of Israel. There were three gates on each side; three on the north side; three on the east side three on the south side; and three on the west side. There were twelve foundation stones and on each stone was written the name of one of the twelve apostles of Christ. So, all 24 elders have their names written on the great city.

"The one who spoke with me had a gold measuring rod to measure the city, and its gates and its wall. The city is laid out as a square, and its length is as great as the width; and he measured the city with the rod, fifteen hundred miles; its length and width and height are equal. And he measured its wall, seventy-two yards, according to human measurements, which are also angelic measurements. The material of the wall was jasper; and the city was pure gold, like clear glass. The foundation stones of the city wall were adorned with every kind of precious stone. The first foundation stone was jasper; the second, sapphire; the third, chalcedony; the fourth, emerald; the fifth, sardonyx; the sixth, sardius; the seventh, chrysolite; the eighth, beryl; the ninth, topaz; the tenth, chrysoprase; the eleventh, jacinth; the twelfth, amethyst. And the twelve gates were twelve pearls; each one of the gates was a single pearl. And the street of the city was pure gold, like transparent glass." (Rev. 21:15-21). John was told to go and measure the city. The city is a perfect cube being fifteen hundred miles in each direction. The wall surrounding the city was seventy-two yards high. This is about as tall as a twenty-one story building. The city is about half the size of the United States of America. Nothing is too good for God's people. The walls are solid jasper adorned with every type of precious stone, the gates are made of pearl and everything in the city is pure gold. Everything is beautiful. The things of this earth that we value highly like gold and precious jewels will be so plentiful that the streets will be paved with gold and the precious gems will be used for building stones.

"I saw no temple in it, for the Lord God the Almighty and the Lamb are its temple. And the city has no need of the sun or of the moon to shine on it, for the glory of God has illumined it, and its lamp is the Lamb. The nations will walk by its light, and the kings of the earth will bring their glory into it. In the daytime (for there will be no night there) its gates will never be closed; and they will bring the glory and the honor of the nations into it; and nothing unclean, and no one who practices abomination and lying, shall ever come into it, but only those whose names are written in the Lamb's book of life." (Rev. 21:22-27). Today we have churches and temples. We have sanctuaries where we can get away and shut the world out so we can worship God. We need a place where we will not be distracted from the things of this world. We need a place where we can feel the very presence of God. There will be no temple in the New Heavens and New Earth. There will be no need for a temple. God and Jesus will be among us. Rather than going to the temple to worship God and Jesus we simply go to God and Jesus themselves and worship Him. There will be no sun or moon to provide light for the city for the glory of God is its light and the Lamb is its lamp. All the nations, people, and all the kings of the earth, the New Earth, are all glorified, and pure and holy. There is no need to close the gates of the city for there is no evil to keep out. Nothing unclean, and no one who practices abominations and lying shall ever come into the city. They have all been destroyed. The only ones who exist on the New Earth are those whose names were written in the Lamb's book of life since the beginning of time.

QUESTIONS CHAPTER 21

Read Revelation 21

1. What is it about?

2. Read Revelation 21:1 Then I saw a New Heaven and a New Earth, Record what the following say

   Isaiah 65:17

   Isaiah 66:22

   2 Peter 3:13

3. What happened to the first heaven and the first earth?

4. What does 2 Peter 3:7, 10 say about this?

5. Does this fulfill what Jesus said as recorded in Matthew 24:35?

Read Revelation 21:2, Hebrews 11:8-10, and Hebrews 11:13-16

6. What do these say about Abraham and the OT saints?

7. Does Revelation 21:2 fulfill what they were looking for?

8. What do you think it means that the New Jerusalem is made ready as a bride adorned for her husband?

9. What is the traditional image of the bride?

Read Revelation 21:3

    10. What is the tabernacle of God?

    11. Who will dwell among the people?

    12. What do the following say:

        John 14:23

        2 Corinthians 6:16

        Leviticus 26:11

        Ezekiel 37:27

    13. Who do the people belong to?

Read Revelation 21:4

    14. What does it say?

    15. How does this compare to:

        Isaiah 25:8

        Isaiah 35:10

        Isaiah 51:11

        Isaiah 65:19

16. What things have passed away?

Read Revelation21:5

17. What does it say?

18. Compare to 2 Corinthians 5:17

19. In context of 2 Corinthians 5:17 what old things pass away and what new things are created?

Read Revelation 21:6

20. What does it say?

21. What does it mean when God refers to Himself as the Alpha and Omega, the beginning and the end?

22. Who can give the water of life?

23. Does this fulfill the prophecy of Isaiah 55:1?

24. Is this the same water Jesus referred to in John 4:10?

25. What is the cost of living water?

Read Revelation 21:7

26. What does it say?

27. What does it mean to be called a son of God?

28. Compare to 2 Samuel 7:14

Read Revelation 21:8, 9

29. What is the destiny of unbelievers?

30. What part do we have in the second death? See Revelation 2:11

Read Revelation 21:10-21

31. Describe the New Jerusalem

Read Revelation 21:22

32. What is the temple?

33. Why do you think there will not be a temple? Think about what the purpose of a temple is.

Read Revelation 21:23

34. Where does the New Jerusalem get its light?

Read Revelation 21:24-26

35. What do the kings and the nations bring into the New Jerusalem?

36. Where did they get it?

Read Revelation 21:27

37. Why is it that nothing unclean and no one who practices abomination and lying shall come into the New Jerusalem?

Chapter 22

The River and Tree of Life

Read Chapter 22 of Revelation

"Then he showed me a river of the water of life, clear as crystal, coming from the throne of God and of the Lamb, in the middle of its street. On either side of the river was the tree of life, bearing twelve kinds of fruit, yielding its fruit every month; and the leaves of the tree were for the healing of the nations". (Rev. 22:1-2). The river of the water of life flows from the throne of God. The source of the living water is God and the Lamb, Jesus. Jeremiah knew about this water and it's source, "For My people have committed two evils: they have forsaken Me, the fountain of living waters, to hew for themselves cisterns, broken cisterns that can hold no water." (Jer. 2:13). God is a fountain of living waters. He has so much living water that it creates a river as it flows from His throne. It flows down through the middle of the street and everyone can drink freely from it. God's people will never forsake Him again. They will never turn away from this living water thinking that they have a source of better water. On either side of the street was the tree of life. The tree was ever bearing, having twelve kinds of fruit. Every month the trees would produce a different kind of fruit. There would never be a time when the trees would be barren. The tree of life first existed in the Garden of Eden. "Then the LORD God said, "Behold, the man has become like one of Us, knowing good and evil; and now, he might stretch out his hand, and take also from the tree of life and eat and live forever." (Gen. 3:22). Man was banished from the Garden of Eden because of his sin. He would no longer have access to the tree of life and live forever. But on the New Earth man has free access to the tree of life and can freely eat of its fruit. This was a promise seen earlier in the book of Revelation. "He who has an ear, let him hear what the Spirit says to the churches. To him who overcomes, I will grant to eat of the tree of life which is in the Paradise of God." (Rev. 2:7). All those who overcome the evils of this world by washing their robes in the blood of the Lamb will have free access to the tree of life. The prophet Ezekiel knew about all of this. "By the river on its bank, on one side and on the other, will grow all kinds of trees for food. Their leaves will not wither and their fruit will not fall. They will bear every month because their water flows from the sanctuary, and their fruit will be for food and their leaves for healing." (Ezek. 47:12).

"There will no longer be any curse; and the throne of God and of the Lamb will be in it, and His bond-servants will serve Him; they will see His face, and His name will be on their foreheads. And there will no longer be any night; and they will not have need of the light of a lamp nor the light of the sun, because the Lord God will illumine them; and they will reign forever and ever." (Rev. 22:3-5). God will never bring His curse upon the earth again. There will be no cause for the curse of God. Everything has been made new. Everything is pure and holy. All evil has been destroyed. All the effects of evil have been destroyed. Man has been reborn pure and holy without blemish. There is nothing to tempt man to sin. Satan, the False Prophet, and the Antichrist have been destroyed. Sin and evil reside in the darkness and there is no darkness. God does not allow anything unholy to be in His presence. The present heavens and earth are full of evil and so God will not make His home on the present earth. Today, God abides with believers through the Holy Spirit. But God will physically abide on the earth in the New Heavens and New Earth. The saints will serve Him and they will see Him face to face. God will no longer be a mysterious force or Spirit which we strive to understand. We will know God as He actually is. His name will be on our foreheads because we belong to Him. We are His people forever and ever. "He has made us to be a kingdom, priests to His God and Father" (Rev. 1:6). We will be priest to God and we will reign over the earth forever and ever. When God created the present earth He created all things. Then, at last, He created man and He gave man dominion over all the things He had created. "Then God said, let us make man in Our image, according to Our likeness; and let them rule over . . . . . all the earth." (Gen. 1:26). Man has now been reborn in the image of God, holy and pure, and righteous and so now has dominion over everything which God has created new. There will never be any darkness again. There will never be any evil again. God's light shines brightly and nothing evil can exist in the light of God.

"And he said to me, "These Words are faithful and true"; and the Lord, the God of the spirits of the prophets, sent His angel to show to His bond-servants the things which must soon take place." (Rev. 22:6). We can believe that everything written in the book of Revelation is true. First, Revelation is a part of the Bible and the Bible is the holy, inspired, infallible, inerrant Word of God. Therefore, Revelation is holy, inspired, infallible, and inerrant. However, in case the reader doesn't understand this, John has written "These Words are faithful and true." We can rely on everything in Revelation as being truth. The Revelation of Jesus Christ was passed on to John by His angel with the express purpose of revealing the things that must take place in order to bring about God's final kingdom.

"And behold, I am coming quickly. Blessed is he who heeds the Words of the prophecy of this book." (Rev. 22:7). Jesus says, "I am coming quickly." These Words were passed on to John almost two thousand years ago now. Jesus has not come yet. Does this negate what He said? In the words of Paul, may it never be! For us mortals who have a finite lifespan of but seventy plus years, two thousand years seems like a very long time. However, in God's time, which is eternal it is but the blink of an eye. No one knows the day or hour of His return but we are to live our lives as though it may be today. There is a blessing for those who heed the words of Revelation. To heed is more than to read or hear. To heed is to pay close attention to what it says. We often hear the word heed used as in "She failed to heed the warning." And in failing to heed the warning she had some adverse thing happen to her. The book of Revelation is a warning of things to come. We do not know the exact time Jesus will return but we are told what is going to happen during the end times. If we read and hear the words of Revelation we will be able to heed the warnings and be prepared. For those who dwell on earth, heeding the warning is to accept Christ as Lord and Savior so they will not be thrown into the lake of fire and burn forever and ever. For those who dwell in heaven the warning is to not fall into temptation and follow the Beast but to persevere through the times, looking forward to the glorious return of Christ and being taken up to be with Him forever and ever.

"I, John, am the one who heard and saw these things. And when I heard and saw, I fell down to worship at the feet of the angel who showed me these things. But he said to me, "Do not do that. I am a fellow servant of yours and of your brethren the prophets and of those who heed the words of this book. Worship God." (Rev. 22:8-9). John testifies that he personally saw and heard these things. He is an eye witness. He is not relating things he heard about from a third person. He actually experienced these things himself. And, having been in the presence of the angel, John fell down before him, believing him to be worthy of worship. The angel corrected him saying he is not to be worshipped, he is a fellow servant of Christ along with John's brothers and those who heed the words of the book of Revelation. We are all equal. The messenger is not greater than the receiver of the message. The prophet is not better than the one who hears the prophecy. There is but One worthy to be worshipped. Worship God.

"And he said to me, "Do not seal up the words of the prophecy of this book, for the time is near. Let the one who does wrong, still do wrong; and the one who is filthy, still be filthy; and let the one who is righteous, still practice righteousness; and the one who is holy, still keep himself holy." (Rev. 22:9-10). The prophecy has been revealed. Write it down for all to read. Don't worry about others. Some will heed the word and some will not. The prophecy has been written for all to read and hear. What they do with it is up to them.

"Behold, I am coming quickly, and My reward is with Me, to render to every man according to what he has done. I am the Alpha and the Omega, the first and the last, the beginning and the end." (Rev. 22:12-13). The time is near. Jesus is coming quickly. When He comes He will bring reward for those who know Him, and judgment for those who don't know Him. There is no middle ground. There is no appeal. Jesus is the first and last. No one and nothing is greater than He. He was, He is, He will come, and He will be forever and ever.

"Blessed are those who wash their robes, so that they may have the right to the tree of life, and may enter by the gates into the city. Outside are the dogs and the sorcerers and the immoral persons and the murderers and the idolaters, and everyone who loves and practices lying." (Rev. 22:14-15). There are two groups of people. There are those who dwell on earth and those who dwell in heaven. Those who dwell on earth do not have access to the tree of life or to the city of God. "The unrighteous will not inherit the kingdom of God. Do not be deceived; neither fornicators, nor idolaters, nor adulterers, nor effeminate, nor homosexuals, nor thieves, nor the covetous, nor drunkards, nor revilers, nor swindlers, will inherit the kingdom of God." (1 Cor. 6:9). Those who dwell in heaven are blessed. These are the ones who have accepted Christ as their Lord and Savior. These no longer wear the filthy robes of sin. "Such were some of you; but you were washed, but you were sanctified, but you were justified in the name of the Lord Jesus Christ and in the Spirit of our God." (1 Cor. 6:11). Your robe has been washed. You have the right to the tree of life. And you have the right to enter the city of God.

"The Spirit and the bride say, "Come." And let the one who hears say, "Come." And let the one who is thirsty come; let the one who wishes take the water of life without cost." (Rev. 22:17). All those who hear the Word are invited to come. All those who thirst after God are invited to come. Anyone who desires to come may come and drink of the water of life without cost.

"I testify to everyone who hears the words of the prophecy of this book: if anyone adds to them, God will add to him the plagues which are written in this book; and if anyone takes away from the words of the book of this prophecy, God will take away his part from the tree of life and from the holy city, which are written in this book." (Rev. 22:18-19). We are clearly warned not to distort the revelation of Jesus Christ. We are not to take away from it and make it out to be less than it is. We are not to add to it and make it out to be more than it is. It is what it is. Those who disobey this warning will find the plagues of this book piled upon them and they will be cut off from the tree of life.

"He who testifies to these things says, "Yes, I am coming quickly." Amen. Come, Lord Jesus. The grace of the Lord Jesus be with all. Amen." (Rev. 22:20-21). This is John's farewell. Jesus says, "Yes I am coming quickly." John says, "Yes! Come, Lord Jesus." And John petitions that the grace of God be with all who read this prophecy. Amen. It is so. There is nothing left to say.

We Win!

QUESTIONS CHAPTER 22

Read Revelation Chapter 22

Read Revelation 22:1,2

1. Where did the river flow from?

2. What do the following say about the source of living waters?

    Jeremiah 2:13

    Jeremiah 17:13

3. Where was the river in relation to the street?

4. What was on either side of the street?

5. How many kinds of trees were there?

6. How many kinds of fruit were there?

7. Will there ever be a time when the tree will not bear fruit?

8. Is this the same tree as in Genesis 2:9?

9. What is the benefit of the tree of life? See Genesis 3:22

10. Who has access to the tree of life? See Revelation 2:7 and 22:14

Read Ezekiel 47:12

    11. Is this the same?

    12. What is the purpose of the leaves?

    13. Are the nations sick? No, All is at peace. As long as there are leaves on the trees which is forever and ever there will be healthy nations.

Read Revelation 22:3, 4

    14. What does this say concerning the curse?

Read Genesis 3:14-19

    15. What was cursed because of the fall of man?

    16. If the curse is removed what will the new condition be?

    17. Who are the bond servants and what will they do?

    18. Why do you think they have the name of Jesus on their foreheads?

Read Revelation 22:5

Read John 12:35-36

Read 1 Thessalonians 5:4-5

Read John 3:19

Read Romans 13:12

Read Ephesians 5:11

    19. Who are those who live in darkness?

    20. What is darkness and what does it do?

    31. If there is no sin or evil will there be any need for darkness?

    32. What will be the source of the light?

    33. Who will reign forever and ever?

Read Revelation22:6

    34. What does this say concerning the book of Revelation?

Read Revelation 22:7

    35. What does it mean to heed the Words of the prophecy of this book?

Read Revelation22:8-9

    36. What is the message conveyed by these verses?

Read Revelation 22:10

    37. Are we to read, study, and encourage others to read and study the book of Revelation?

Read Revelation 22:11

    38. Are we to worry and fret over others?

    39. Who must we be concerned about?

Read Revelation 22:12

    40. What will Jesus render to the wicked?

    41. What will Jesus render to the righteous?

Read Revelation22:13

    42. What does this say about Jesus?

    43. What does it say about His eternal state?

    44. What does it say about His dominion?

    45. What does it say about His authority?

    46. What does it say about His power?

Read Revelation 22:14

    47. What does it mean to wash one's robe?

Read Revelation 22:15

Read Matthew 8:11-12

48. What does this say concerning the unrighteous?

Read 1 Corinthians 6:9-10

49. What does this say concerning the unrighteous?

Read Revelation 22:16

50. How does this describe Jesus?

Read Revelation 22:17

51. What is this an invitation to?

Read Revelation 22:18-19

52. What is this a warning about?

53. What does Revelation 1:3 say?

54. What can we conclude from this?

Read Revelation 22:20-21

Yes, Jesus is coming quickly. The grace of the Lord Jesus be with all of you. Amen and Amen.

Summary

The book of Revelation is the climax of the Bible. Everything from Genesis 1:1 to Jude 1:25 has its purpose fulfilled in the book of Revelation. Without the book of Revelation the rest of the book doesn't make sense. All of the prophecies of Scripture have been fulfilled except for those related to the end of time. There are end time prophecies throughout Scripture but the book of Revelation is a book set aside for the express purpose of giving us understanding concerning the end of time. It is, "The revelation of Jesus Christ, which God gave Him to show His bondservants, the things which must soon take place . . . " (Rev. 1:1). It is God's desire that we know what will take place.

It is God's purpose to amass for Himself a people who will be His people and live through all eternity with Him in a world He will create that is perfect, holy, pure, and undefiled. In order to accomplish His purpose, all evil and the effects of evil must be destroyed. The present heavens and earth are not suitable for God's people. They have been defiled by sin and cursed by God. For this reason the present world has storms, floods, and earthquakes that bring destruction, insects that bite and destroy crops, weeds that choke out our gardens, wild animals and reptiles that threaten life, sickness and death, pain and suffering, hatred and bitterness, greed and lust, and people who will do anything to raise themselves above the rest of mankind. None of this is fit and acceptable for the kingdom of God.

God is a fair and just God. God sets the rules and condition by which we are to live. In essence these rules are simply to love God with all your heart mind and soul and to love your neighbor as yourself. Those who obey the rules will be blessed and have eternal life those who refuse to obey the rules will reap the wrath of God and will die. When God created man He gave him free will. Man could choose to obey God or defy God. Satan tempted man in the Garden of Eden and man chose to listen to Satan rather than obey God. Man was removed from the Garden of Eden and was excluded from access to the tree of life. The earth was cursed with weeds, storms, earthquakes, and things that destroy life and property and make life hard for man. Man was cursed by having to work hard for a living and being subject to pain, suffering and sickness. Satan was cursed, having to spend his days crawling around in the filth of the earth.

Adam was created in the image of God. However, he had the free will to choose to do good or do evil. Adam chose to do evil. Thus the image of God in Adam was shattered. "When Adam had lived one hundred and thirty years, he became the father of a son in his own likeness, according to his image, and named him Seth." (Gen. 5:3). All of present day mankind come from Seth. Seth was not born in the image of God but was born in the image of sinful Adam. "All have sinned and fall short of the glory of God." (Rom. 3:23) There is no opportunity for eternal life through perfect obedience to the Law. It is impossible. Therefore all deserve death and the wrath of God. However, what man could not do, God did. As man was incapable of perfectly obeying the Law, God sent His Son to this earth to live a perfect life and earn the right to suffer and die for the sins of His people. His death redeemed those bound for destruction if they would simply believe in Him. "For by grace you have been saved through faith; and that not of yourselves, it is the gift of God." (Eph. 2:8). "He saved us, not on the basis of deeds which we have done in righteousness, but according to His mercy, by the washing of regeneration and renewing by the Holy Spirit, whom He poured out upon us richly through Jesus Christ our Savior." (Titus 3:4-6). Salvation comes through faith in our Lord Jesus Christ, knowing that He gave Himself up on the cross in our place and in doing so has cleansed us of all sin and unrighteousness. And the faith is not of our own doing it is imparted to us through the work of the Holy Spirit.

Those who have been saved through faith have been born again with a new spirit. "But now we have been released from the Law, having died to that by which we were bound, so that we serve in newness of the Spirit and not in oldness of the letter." (Rom.7:6). "But now having been freed from sin and enslaved to God, you derive your benefit, resulting in sanctification, and the outcome, eternal life." (Rom. 6:22). So, those who have been saved through faith have been freed from sin, are enslaved to

God and are sanctified and made holy. They are now fit for eternal life in God's kingdom. The rest must go to destruction.

The present heavens and earth are not fit for the kingdom of God. None of mankind, except those who are saved through faith, are fit for the kingdom of God. And Satan, the tempter, who tempted Eve in the Garden of Eden is not fit for the kingdom of God. God must destroy all evil and the effects of evil and recreate all things new. Therefore, the present heavens and earth must be destroyed, all mankind, except those who have been saved, must be destroyed, and Satan and his angels must be destroyed.

The book of Revelation shows exactly how God will go about destroying all evil and recreating a New Heaven and New Earth in which His kingdom will be established and in which we will live with Him forever and ever. In the book of Revelation the Antichrist appears. He comes on the scene and brings peace for Israel. He arranges for the temple to be rebuilt. And then after three and a half years he stands in the temple and declares himself to be god. He demands that all people everywhere bow down to him. No one is allowed to buy or sell unless they have his mark. Following his declaration that he is god there will be three and a half years of great tribulation. At the end of this time the saints will be removed from the earth. Then God's wrath will be poured out upon the earth. There will be a great battle at Armageddon. All the people on earth will come against Jesus and His army of saints and all will die except the saints. The False Prophet and the Antichrist will be thrown into the lake of fire. Satan will be bound in the Abyss for a thousand years. During the thousand years the saints will reign with Jesus on the present earth. After the thousand years are completed Satan will be released and the dead will be resurrected. Satan will gather the resurrected dead together and will march them to Jerusalem to attempt to take over the world. Fire and brimstone will rain down on them and they will all die. Satan will be thrown into the lake of fire where the False Prophet and Antichrist are. The dead will be judged and will be thrown into the lake of fire also. Then the heavens and earth will be disintegrated with intense heat and a New Heavens and New Earth will appear. The city of God, the New Jerusalem, will come down out of heaven. All the saints will inhabit the New Jerusalem and we will walk the streets of gold side by side with Jesus. We will see and talk with God face to face. There will be no more pain, no more suffering, and no more heart aches, these have all passed away and we will remember them no more.

In a nutshell, We Win!

EPILOGUE

It is done! This has been over a year in the writing. During this time I have seen a wonderful new world open up before my eyes. There are many mysteries in the Old and New Testaments that can only be understood when viewed through the eyes of the book of Revelation. It is when we accept God's Word as truth from beginning to end that He opens Scripture for our understanding. I hope I have been faithful to my purpose to bring to the reader a literal interpretation of the book of Revelation without embellishment. If I have added to or taken away anything from the book of Revelation, may God forgive me. My intent was to be as true to Scripture as possible. And so it has now been presented to you.

I have been much blessed in this endeavor and I hope you, too, have been much blessed in your study of the book of Revelation.

Come quickly Lord Jesus!

"The grace of the Lord Jesus be with all. Amen." (Revelation 22:21)

About The Author

The author, Reverend Barry F. Brinson studied religion and theology for five years at Emory University and served as pastor of two churches in Holly Hill, SC for eight years. Barry is a devout Christian who loves to discover the truth of God's Word. He believes that God's Word is holy, inspired, infallible and inerrant. And, further it is his belief that when one accepts Scripture as truth then God begins to open His Word for understanding and when one denies Scripture truth then God closes the door to understanding. Barry is now retired from the ministry and has devoted much of his time to study and teaching. Barry is married and he and his wife celebrated their 50th wedding anniversary in 2011. As of this writing he has three children, eight grandchildren and two great grand children.

APPENDIX

End Times Timeline

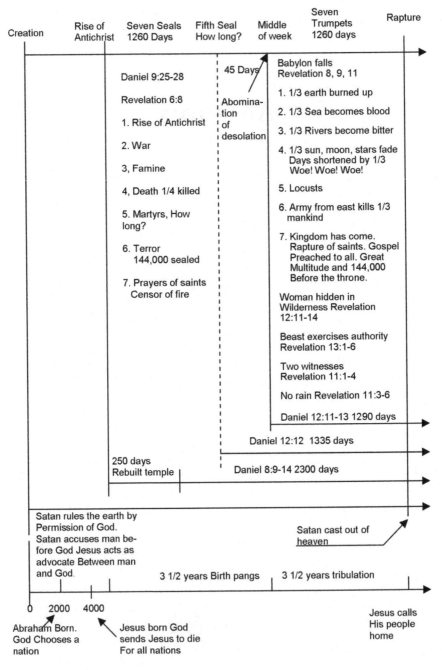

Creation | **Rise of Antichrist** | **Seven Seals 1260 Days** | **Fifth Seal How long?** | **Middle of week** | **Seven Trumpets 1260 days** | **Rapture**

45 Days

Babylon falls
Revelation 8, 9, 11

Daniel 9:25-28

1. 1/3 earth burned up

Revelation 6:8

Abomination of desolation

2. 1/3 Sea becomes blood

1. Rise of Antichrist

3. 1/3 Rivers become bitter

2. War

4. 1/3 sun, moon, stars fade
   Days shortened by 1/3
   Woe! Woe! Woe!

3, Famine

4, Death 1/4 killed

5. Locusts

5. Martyrs, How long?

6. Army from east kills 1/3 mankind

6. Terror
   144,000 sealed

7. Kingdom has come.
   Rapture of saints. Gospel
   Preached to all. Great
   Multitude and 144,000
   Before the throne.

7. Prayers of saints
   Censor of fire

Woman hidden in
Wilderness Revelation
12:11-14

Beast exercises authority
Revelation 13:1-6

Two witnesses
Revelation 11:1-4

No rain Revelation 11:3-6

Daniel 12:11-13 1290 days

Daniel 12:12 1335 days

250 days
Rebuilt temple

Daniel 8:9-14 2300 days

Satan rules the earth by
Permission of God.
Satan accuses man be-
fore God Jesus acts as
advocate Between man
and God.

Satan cast out of
heaven

3 1/2 years Birth pangs

3 1/2 years tribulation

0   2000   4000

Abraham Born.
God Chooses a
nation

Jesus born God
sends Jesus to die
For all nations

Jesus calls
His people
home

End Times Timeline (Continued)

Rapture

Six Bowls 30 days	Armageddon	Seventh Bowl	Millennium 1000 years	Final Battle	New heaven New earth
					► Eternity
Revelation 16	Jesus comes with His army of saints	Revelation 16:17	Satan bound For 1000 Years Revelation 20:1-3	Satan released Revelation 20:7	New heaven and New earth Revelation 21:1-9
1. Sores	Beast is seized	It is done		Unsaved dead rise to follow Satan into battle Revelation 20:5,8	
2. Everything in sea dies	False Prophet seized		Saints come alive to reign with Christ Revelation 20:4		New Jeru-salem Revelation 20:10-27
3. Waters become blood	Rest are killed				
4. Sun scorches men	No one is left Revelation 19:20-21		Rest remain dead during the 1000 years Revelation 20:5	Satan gathers his army and they attack Jerusalem Revelation 20:8-9	We live with Christ forever and ever
5. Kingdom of beast darkened				God de-stroys them Revelation 20:9	
6. Euphrates dries up			Holy place properly restored		
				Satan thrown into the lake of fire where the Anti-christ and False Prophet are Revelation 20:10	
				White throne judgment Revelation 20:11-15	

Jesus rules. Satan has lost his power over the saints. The ingathering of the saints is complete.

► Eternity

---

30 Days of God's wrath

Millennium

► Eternity

1000 years

↙ Jesus calls His people home

↖ All evil removed from the earth

↙ Great white throne judgment. All evil destroyed.